THE
DAY THE
NUMBERS
SPOKE

THE DAY THE NUMBERS SPOKE

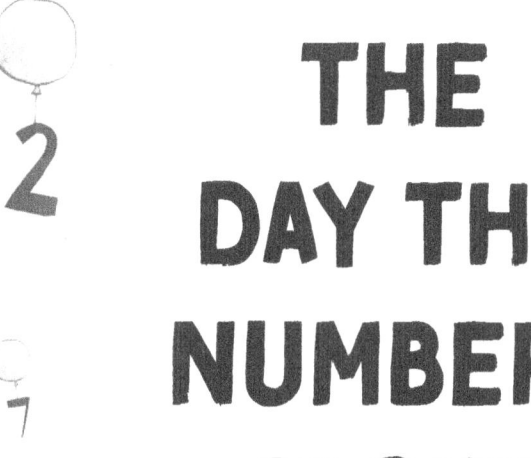

POEMS BY JOHN AGARD
ILLUSTRATED BY SATOSHI KITAMURA

HODDER CHILDREN'S BOOKS

Content previously published in *Einstein, The Girl Who Hated Maths* in 2002,
Hello H2O in 2003, and *The Rainmaker Danced* in 2017
This edition first published in 2024 by Hodder & Stoughton

SRD

A CIP catalogue record for this book is available from the British Library.

ISBN 978 1 444 97546 8

Printed and bound in India by Manipal Technologies Limited, Manipal

The paper and board used in this book
are made from wood from responsible sources.

MIX
Paper | Supporting
responsible forestry
FSC™ C104740

Hodder Children's Books
An imprint of
Hachette Children's Group
Part of Hodder & Stoughton Limited
Carmelite House
50 Victoria Embankment
London EC4Y 0DZ

An Hachette UK Company
www.hachette.co.uk

www.hachettechildrens.co.uk

CONTENTS

EINSTEIN, THE GIRL WHO HATED MATHS

HELLO H20

THE RAINMAKER DANCED

EINSTEIN, THE GIRL
WHO HATED MATHS

Einstein

The Girl Who Hated Maths

Her parents liked the name
so they called her Einstein.
And how she hated maths.
She'd rather play with cats
or do a drawing of the sunshine.

But they made her count from one to nine
and put one in front of zero.
Ten, they said, would follow.
But it wasn't as much fun
as snowballing in the snow.

So her maths homework never gets done
without a whinge and whine
from that girl Einstein.
She thinks maths is a pain.
Too many numbers nibbling at her brain.

1

Whoever invented maths
must have been out of their mind.
All those funny little signs
swarming like splodges of ink.
What is Einstein supposed to think?

She didn't really care
that two matching items make a pair
so four pairs of shoes are four times two –
as long as she got to choose
her favourite party-blue.

Two pairs of feet fit four roller skates,
how many pairs of feet fit eight?
'Ah,' sighs Einstein, 'why don't we migrate
to a country where there's no maths.
Tell me and I'll jump on a jet.'

Well, Einstein, wherever you jet-set
– Africa, Europe, India, Tibet –
numbers will greet you on arrival
like letters of the alphabet.
Numbers too are a way of survival.

Yes, wherever you go, maths will follow.
But don't worry, numbers are fine,
her parents would say to their Einstein.
Both were accountants by profession,
though once her dad made a confession.

'Of all the subjects, I must admit
maths was not my favourite.
I was near the bottom of the class.
How do you think I managed to pass?
Ask your mum and she will tell you.'

'Well,' said her mum, 'I've told you before.
Dad was the boy who lived next door.
And I helped him with his maths homework.
Maths, you could say, was our matchmaker
and that was long before calculators.'

It was maths that brought them together.
It was numbers that made their love shine
– they were thirteen at the time –
until one day, six years later,
into the world came cuddly Einstein.

'So,' Einstein said smiling, 'that would mean
I was born when you were nineteen.'
'Right,' said her mum, 'nine times two plus one.'
'Or ten times two less one,' said her dad.
'You see, Einstein, maths isn't that bad.

'Like your two cats, weren't they an addition
to the family?' And Einstein agreed
two cats were two extra mouths to feed.
And her cats soon had six kittens - no lying -
for cats have a way of multiplying.

That meant finding homes for twelve, one by one,
and their going was sad subtraction.
Of course, Einstein got into a mood,
but since cats have nine lives, she knew
her two cats would have nine times two.

'Eighteen,' said Mum, 'that's a lot of lives.'
And she told Einstein a brain-teaser
'Sounds tricky, but nothing's easier.
Now this will test your grasp of digits.
Five cats catch five mice in five minutes.

'How many cats would you need
to catch 100 mice in 100 minutes?
Take your time, Einstein. Don't answer yet,
for it's a question with a catch.
Remember, the mice and minutes match.'

Those same five cats, if they're feeling fit,
would catch 60 mice in 60 minutes
would catch 100 mice in 100 minutes.
The answer was five, Einstein knew it.
And isn't it fun when numbers play tricks?

Without numbers we'd have no address.
The poor postman would be in a mess.
Numbers help us to communicate.
Without them we'd be lost for a birthday date
or how many candles to put on the cake.

Counting began with fingers and toes.
Some even did sums on knuckles and elbows.
Do you know two hands could add up to a billion?
Now we take for granted the gift of zero –
the egg that hatches tens into trillions.

Long, long ago it was the abacus.
Now calculators do our counting for us.
But pebbles, bones, shells and sticks
all played their part in mathematics.
'Numbers,' said her mum and dad, 'make music.'

And sure as flower petals come in fives
like the points of stars in the skies,
Einstein began to feel maths come alive.
And while Mum and Dad clicked their fingers,
Einstein tapped her feet to the beat of numbers.

Keeping Fit

Forget aerobics and gymnastics.
I'm keeping fit with mathematics.
None of this jogging lark
and malarky round the park.

I burn up calories
swivelling my shoulder
three hundred and sixty degrees.
I become a circle
turning on two bent knees.

Now it's doubles and trebles
with toes and knuckles.
I multiply inbreath
by outbreath.
That usually works up a sweat.

Now watch me extend my arms
into parallelograms.
With a twist of the torso
I squat like a zero.
Then to test my flexibility

I stretch and stretch and stretch

to infinity.

How Many Is How Many?

How many stars make a sky?
How many waves make a sea?

How many sands make a beach?
How many leaves make a tree?

How many trees make a forest?
How many drops make a rainfall?

Whatever number you guess
will always seem kind of small,

for a billion sounds like a lot
to the ears of an earthling,

but to galaxies spiralling
a billion is only a dot.

.100000

Depending
on its spot
it can lessen
what you've got.

It reduces
the highest
number
to rock-bottom.

Can make even
a million
seem less
than a lot.

All power
to the dot.
the dot.
the dot.

The Day the Numbers Spoke

Number one said:
Where I'm going, I go alone.
That is me, myself and I.

Number two said:
I'm part of a perfect couple
and we're heading for the sky.

Number three said:
I've had enough of triangles
O to be a circle for a while.

Number four said:
North, South, East, West, I'm all about,
At home in every direction.

Number five said:
Simply gaze at a single star
and I'll twinkle my reflection.

Number six said:
My fortune takes me far and wide
for I'm the top throw on the dice.

Number seven said:
To the heavens that's where I'll go.
Look no higher than a rainbow.

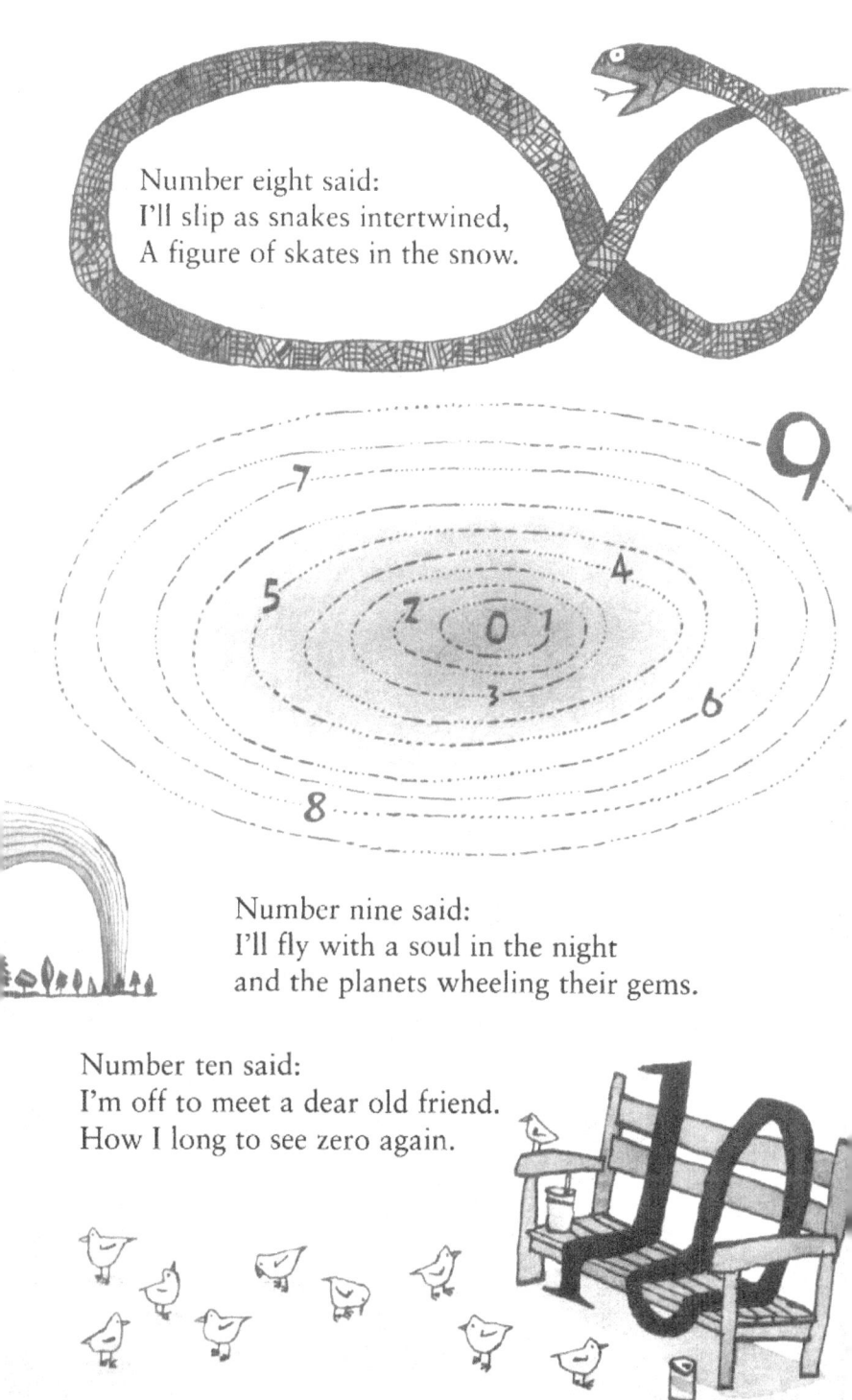

Number eight said:
I'll slip as snakes intertwined,
A figure of skates in the snow.

Number nine said:
I'll fly with a soul in the night
and the planets wheeling their gems.

Number ten said:
I'm off to meet a dear old friend.
How I long to see zero again.

0

Zero
you mischievous
goblin nought
that can make
a number grow

into hundreds
into thousands
into millions
into billions
into trillions
into zillions

and on
and on
into a forever
horizon
where a glimpse is caught
of naughty nought
rolling like an egg
that's pleased with itself
because little nought knows
that multiplied by zero
the biggest zillion
returns to
zero.

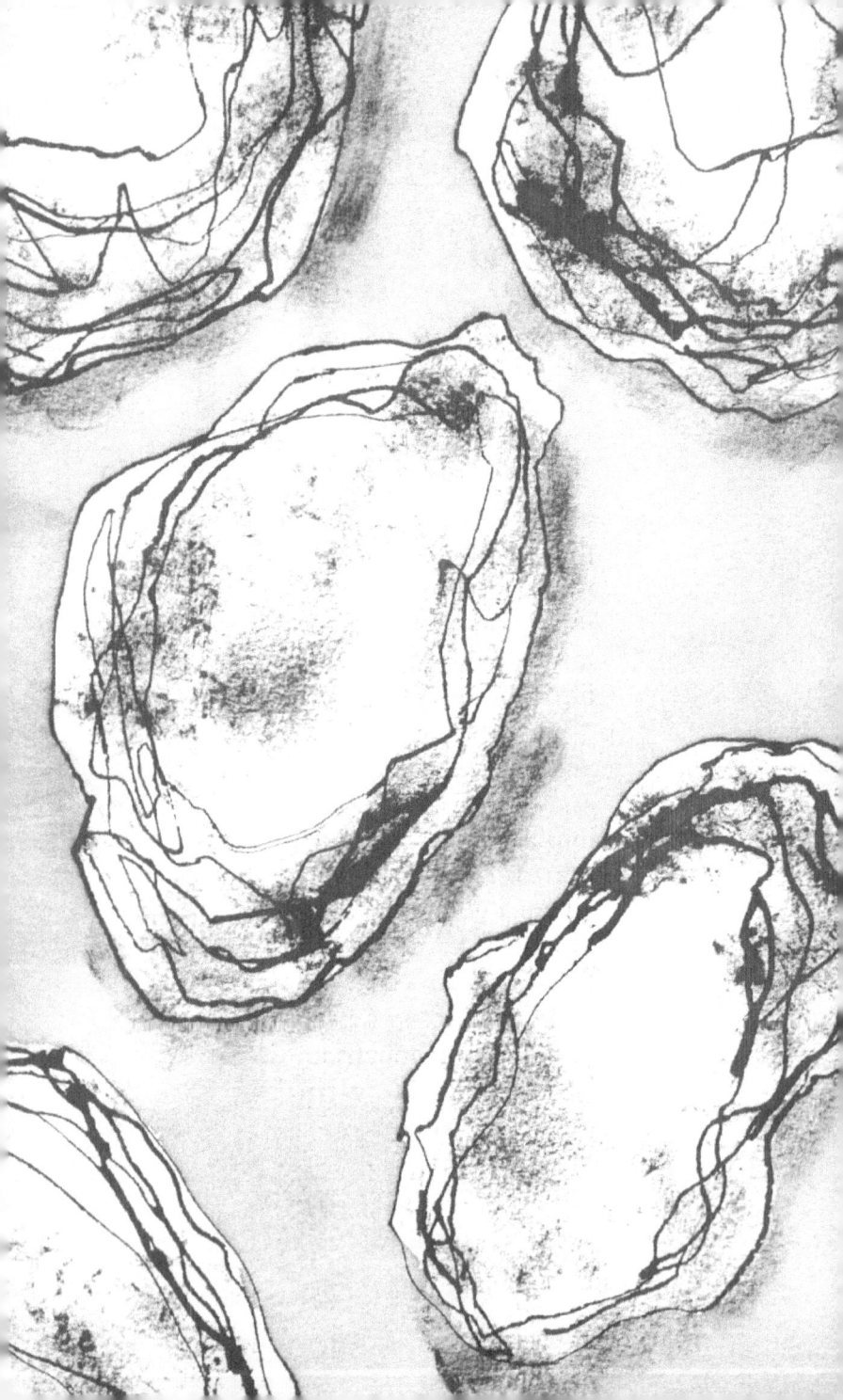

Oyster Girl

They call me Oyster Girl
And I'm at home in sea world.

I skip among coral.
I hopscotch on seaweed.
Under a moon that's full
I play You-Follow-I-Lead.

Remember, all you who stand
and gaze at the sea,
Oysters there are many
but in every thousand

You'll find only one pearl
And that's me, Oyster Girl.

A Wonderful 100 Per Cent

Since my body
is 70 per cent water,
same as planet earth,
it's no wonder
when I cry
and when I laugh
streams flow from my eyes,
and when I do a wee
I become a little fountain,
and when I perspire
I'm all river
and every vein
a running tributary.

But what of the other
30 per cent of me?
O my bones are minerals,
my teeth undiscovered gems.
Let me just say in all modesty,
I'm a wonderful 100 per cent.

The Mental Arithmetic Twist

It's a new dance groove, goes like this,
it's the Mental Arithmetic Twist.

Twist your brain cells round addition,
tune in to the plus–plus rhythm.

You don't need a calculator
to be a counting operator.

What's a million but one and six zeroes,
and you've got ten fingers and ten toes.

And since a million's ten to the power of six,
you can snap and tap and shake your hips.

Yeah do the Mental Arithmetic Twist.
Can you dig it? Can you jig it?

An Ark, An Ark

An Ark, an Ark,
Noah shall make
for when the skies shall grow dark
and the thunder shall shake.

Three hundred cubits
of length he shall give it.
Fifty cubits
of width he shall give it.
Thirty cubits
of height he shall give it.

Better start building quick.
But Brother Noah is losing his wits.
The poor man no good at arithmetic.

Ishango Bone

Ishango Bone
how old are you
and what did you do
and where were you from
before this museum?
I've so many questions.
Ishango Bone
are you really
8000 years old? Who knows?
And was your home
a lake that flows
into the River Nile
high in the mountains
of Central Africa?

Ishango Bone
before you became
an object to be gazed at,
did those notches
row by row
help the Ishango
to add and subtract
and mark the phases
of the moon?

Ishango Bone,
one last question.
This calculator
that helps me with my maths –
will it like you
become an artefact?

Who Will Grieve
for Forty Thieves

Forty thieves
Forty thieves
O who will grieve
for forty thieves?

Not I said Ali Baba
You'll have to look far to find badder.

Not I said the judge
The scales of justice will not budge.

Not I said the rich man
They stole my gold and away they ran.

Forty thieves
Forty thieves
O who will grieve
for forty thieves?

I will said a voice from a cave
I will grieve for forty thieves.
I who open at Open Sesame
grieve for all who enter eternity.

 Day Keeper

Day keeper
Day keeper
Where do you keep days?

Do you dissolve them in rivers of sleep?
Do you scatter them for the winds to reap?

Day keeper
Day keeper
Where do you keep days?

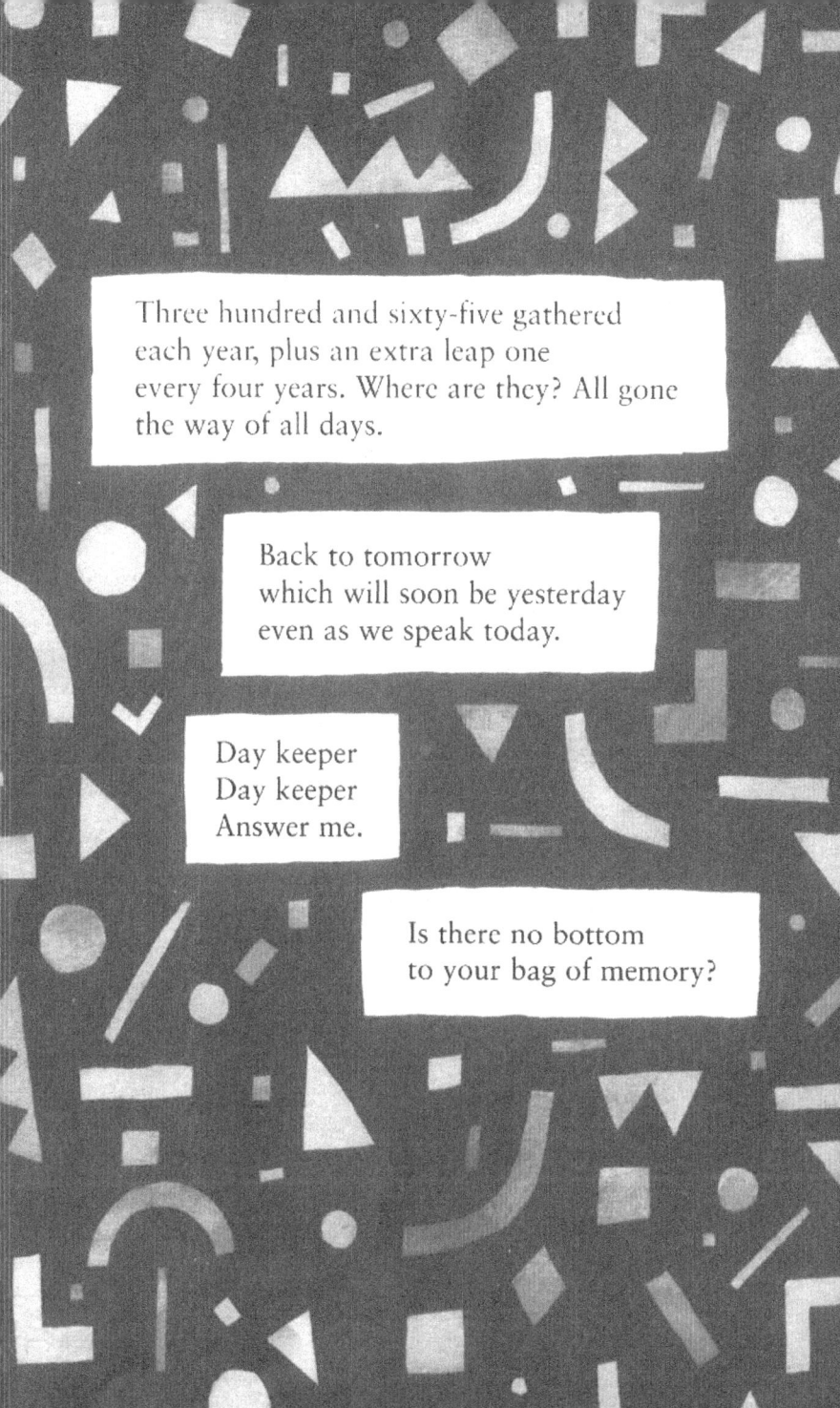

Three hundred and sixty-five gathered
each year, plus an extra leap one
every four years. Where are they? All gone
the way of all days.

Back to tomorrow
which will soon be yesterday
even as we speak today.

Day keeper
Day keeper
Answer me.

Is there no bottom
to your bag of memory?

The Polygons

Polly Polygon
and Peter Polygon
lived all their lives
bounded by straight lines.

And down at the club
of curves and squiggles,
members had a giggle
at the straight-lined couple,
for polygons weren't welcome.

'O, can't be much fun
being a polygon,
how we'd hate to be straight.'

'On the contrary,'
said Mr and Mrs Polygon.
'We haven't a single complaint.

'For we party with pentagons,
hobnob with hexagons
and spend quality time
with quadrilaterals.
We're party animals.

'And once in moonlit Havana
we danced the rhombus
to sounds of the rhumba.
All our lives we've been straight
and we've managed quite well
without any curves and bends.

'Mind you,' said the Polygons,
'We do have a wide circle of friends.'

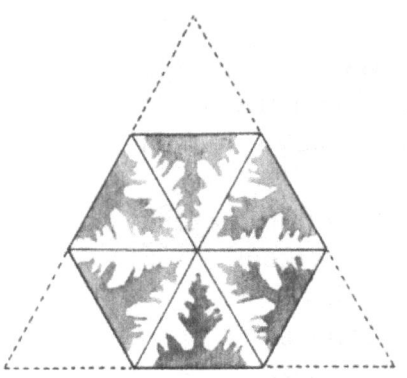

Once Upon An Equilateral Triangle

An equilateral triangle
grew tired of being equilateral.
No, I want to live life to the full.
It's all right having sixty degrees
in every pocket of my angles,
but I'd rather take off in a breeze,
footloose as a bird or a bee.
I wonder if I can wangle
myself into some new form or shape.
So the equilateral triangle
divided each of its sides into thirds
and did a little whirl and a swirl.
It was geometry in motion.
Suddenly, something special occurred.
With a final spin and a shake,
the triangle changed to a hexagon,
taking the form of, guess what? A snowflake.

On Cloud Nine

On cloud nine
everything's fine

nothing's ever
at sixes and sevens

on cloud nine
all is heaven.

Everybody goes about
in Sunday best

people are dressed
to the nines

on cloud nine
everywhere is a song

and one gets along with one.

Quipu Chant

By coloured knots on strings,
we Keepers of the Knots
we remember
our Inca beginnings.

By the Quipu, our calendar.
By the Quipu, our ledger.
By the Quipu, our message-bearer.

By the counting threads
of the Quipu,
we Keepers of the Knots
we account for
the ears of corn
the heads of cattle
the gold of the sun
the silver of the moon
the roaming llama.

By the living threads
of the Quipu,
we Keepers of the Knots
we account for
the fallen in battle,
the numbers gone to Pachacamac
god of earth and time,
and the numbers still here
to breathe rain's miracle.

By the talking threads
of the Quipu,
we Keepers of the Knots
we keep the past un-dead.
We who unravel
the Quipu's secrets
as the hours unravel us.
We Keepers of the Knots.
Let it not be said
that we forgot.

Triskaidekaphobia

TRISKAIDEKAPHOBIA? What does it mean?
It's when someone's scared of number 13.
But how can a number be scary?
Don't ask me, ask the dictionary.

Archimedes' Mother Speaks to the Press

I knew he'd follow
a mathematical path.
Don't ask how. Mums just know.
Besides, he always spent
such a long time in the bath,
tracing spirals and segments
on his olive-oiled skin.

It became a family joke –
the way he would toy with the soap,
calculating its volume,
testing its equilibrium.
You could say I was a patient Mum.
By the time he'd stepped from the bath,
he was glistening
with parabolas,
or so he called them.
I just knew when I heard the news
of someone running stark naked
through the streets of Syracuse –
some mathematician
according to rumour –

I just knew it could only be
my Archie,
my bath-loving doodler,
running in the altogether,
inviting the world to join him
in his EUREKA, EUREKA.

The Soul from Different Angles

The soul is a spiral,
said the first mathematician.
A shell awakening from sleep.

The soul is a straight line,
said the second mathematician.
An arrow that pierces deep.

The soul is a triangle,
said the third mathematician.
The unity of three in one.

The soul is a square,
said the fourth mathematician.
Each side a benediction.

The soul is a circle,
said the fifth mathematician.
A wheel forever turning.

How shall I put it?
said the last mathematician,
The soul is anybody's guess.

But I'd like to suggest
the soul is an egg
holding itself within itself.

You Isosceles

Please.
I didn't mean to be rude
when I called you Isosceles.
It's not some kind of disease.
Honest.
Just the way your trousers dangle
with your legs apart –
reminds me of a triangle
with two sides of equal length
and your shoes
two equal angles
that could do with a shining.
Never mind my shoes,
You Hypothenuse.

ImproperFractions

Just because our numerator
is bigger than
our denominator
is no excuse
for calling us
improper.
Don't make us laugh!
Let $^{15}/_2$
be rewritten
as $7\,^1/_2$.
This gives a fraction
great satisfaction
and we like to think
it's a proper
transaction.

Bisector

They call me Bisector.
That's what I do best. Bisect.
And I'm no respecter
of angle or line.
I'll bisect them any time.
Bisecting is my line.

They call me Bisector.
The mean mediator.
The perky perpendicular.
I may sound like a bully
but deep down I'm a softie.
I believe in equality.

So I bisect an angle
into equal parts, only fair,
and each one gets an equal share.
I bisect right, I bisect left,
I even bisect myself.
That's, of course, my greatest test.

Number 9 Would Like A Word

Take any number.
Multiply by 9.
The answer combined
will add up to 9.
O isn't it divine
to be number 9?

The number of stitches
that could be saved
by a stitch in time.
The number of twists
to Hell's river Styx.
The number of steps
to Heaven's City.

The number of branches
on the cosmic tree.
The number of Muses
to give inspiration.
The number of heads
on a Chinese dragon.
The number of months
for a baby to arrive.
The number of lives
permitted a cat.
And I'll tell you what,
I Number 9
feel even more divine
when dressed up to the nines.

A Beeline as the Crow Flies

How do you travel
the shortest distance
between two points?
Would you do a zig-zag prance?

The bee knows but says nothing.
Just makes a honeybeeline
from flower to flower
in a dance of nectar.

The crow knows but says nothing.
Just joins earth to sky
in an embrace of near and far.
As the crow flies, as the crow flies.

I know.
Just make a beeline for the fridge
where the ice-cream's cool,
then fly like a crow to my room.

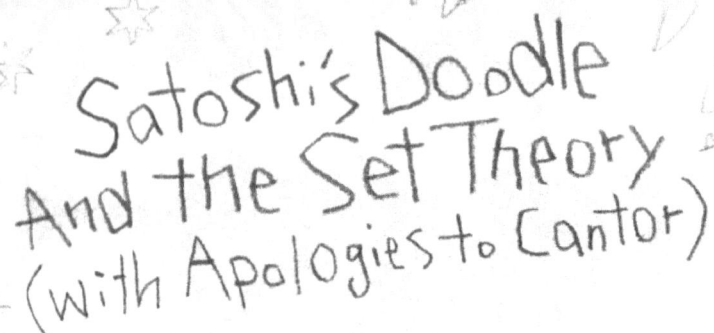

Satoshi's Doodle
And the Set Theory
(with Apologies to Cantor)

MR GEORG CANTOR

MR AGARD

Settle down, Satoshi.
And pay attention.
Well, class, are we set
for the Set Theory?

Just pretend
you've got a set of three
apples in a bowl.
Let apple one be paired
with the number 1.
Let apple two be paired
with the number 2.
Let apple three be paired
with the number 3.
Now let each be squared.
What's that? I hear you ask.
An impossible task.
Can a round apple
be possibly squared?

Oh yes, down to the core,
as two times two make four,
for a number squared
is that by itself multiplied
as three times three make nine
and nine times nine – eighty-one.
We can go on and on and on
and yet,
and yet no nearer, a glimpse
of that number beyond the beyond.

Let me put it like this.
Since one apple holds
all the appleness
of a set in a bowl –
which is a little universe –
then an apple forever squared
multiplies its appleness
more times than can be told,
as your doodle, Satoshi,
simply by being forever squared
can multiply its doodleness
into a galaxy
of never-ending doodles.

But enough of the Set Theory.
Tomorrow we do sub-sets,
which are sets within sets.
Meanwile, here's a tongue-twister
to tease your mind-sets.

Henny Penny, the setting hen,
on a nest of three eggs squared three times round.
How many eggs in the setting sun
Did Henny Penny actually sit upon?

Animal Arithmetic

What's a herd of cows
to a cow?

What's a flock of sheep
to a sheep?

What's a pack of wolves
to a wolf?

What's a gang of geese
to a goose?

Animals, they say, are no good
at arithmetic?

Mother Hen doesn't agree –
scurrying from her nest
stirring up a fuss
scratching the dust
for that one minus

her missing egg.

The Weight of Words

Diplodocus
weighed 11 tons.

Brontosaurus
weighed 30 tons.

Brachiosaurus
weighed 100 tons.

Tyrannosaurus
the fiercest of all
weighed only 6 1/2 tons.

Where are they now
these terribly spectacular lizards?

O if only they had known
the weight of words
in my Roget's Thesaurus,
which doesn't weigh much,

they might have told their own
story for us.

A Mountain of a Heart

We elephants have a heart
that weighs 48 pounds –
more than 20 kilograms.
A mountain of a beast
deserves a mountain of a heart.

And when we hug trunk-to-trunk,
it's a larger than life cuddle.
And when two elephants bask
in the goodness of water splashed,
our grey flanks shine with knowing

that a heart weighs as much as love lets it.

No Bananas Among No Monkeys

Three bananas among three monkeys.
How many does each monkey receive?

One.

A thousand bananas among a thousand monkeys.
How many does each monkey receive?

One.

But there at the back of the class
one little boy raised a finger
with a burning question to ask.

'What if no bananas
were divided among no monkeys?'

The whole class found it funny.
They thought, it's only Ramanujan –
for this was the boy's name –
being a mischievous Hanuman
with another one of his games.

But from the teacher's expression
it was a serious question
that young Ramanujan had proposed.

'Well done, Ramanujan,
you've taken us far beyond
the world of zeros.
No bananas among no monkeys
has baffled maths minds for centuries.'

Fermat Expostulates His Last Margin to an Intruder

Don't you know you should knock
before entering?

You can't just barge in
while I'm working in the margin.

It's a sign of good gumption
to propose an assumption

and leave others to imagine
and ponder the proof.

So I'll scribble in the margin
$X^n + Y^n = Z^n$.

That should keep them guessing.
Yes, I'll have them all goofed.

Just between you and me,
of course the margin's wide enough

for sums of squares and cubes
and to prove what's what of my theory.

So in my grave I'll have the last laugh.
Here lies Fermat who lied

to keep the margin marvellous.

Recipe for a Magic Square

A yellow river.

A Chinese emperor.

A turtle's back.

Odd

Two odd numbers
always add up
to an even.

But two even numbers
never add up
to an odd.

We odd numbers
like to think we're
the handiwork of God.

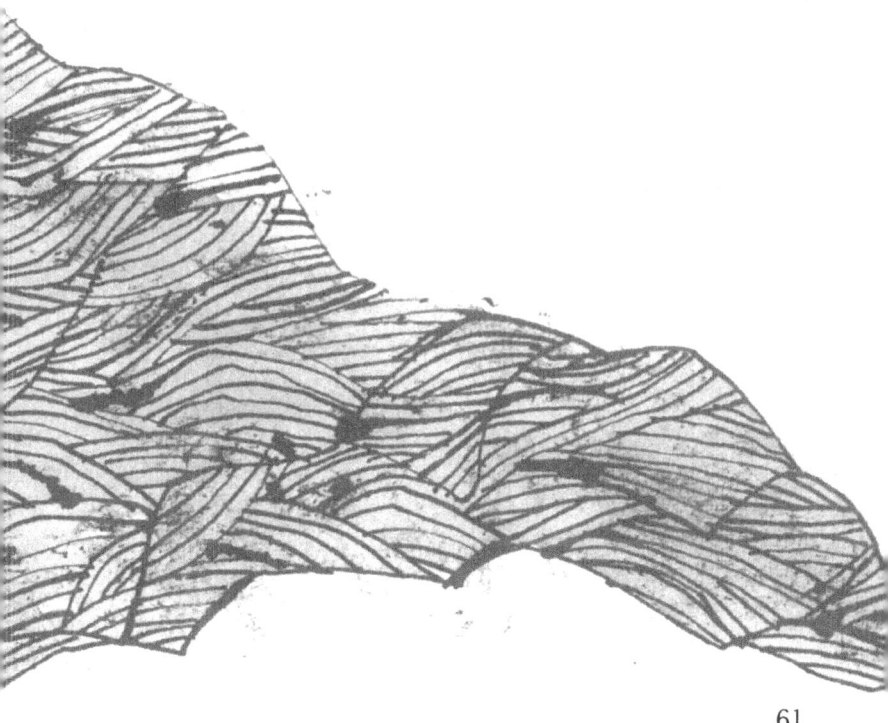

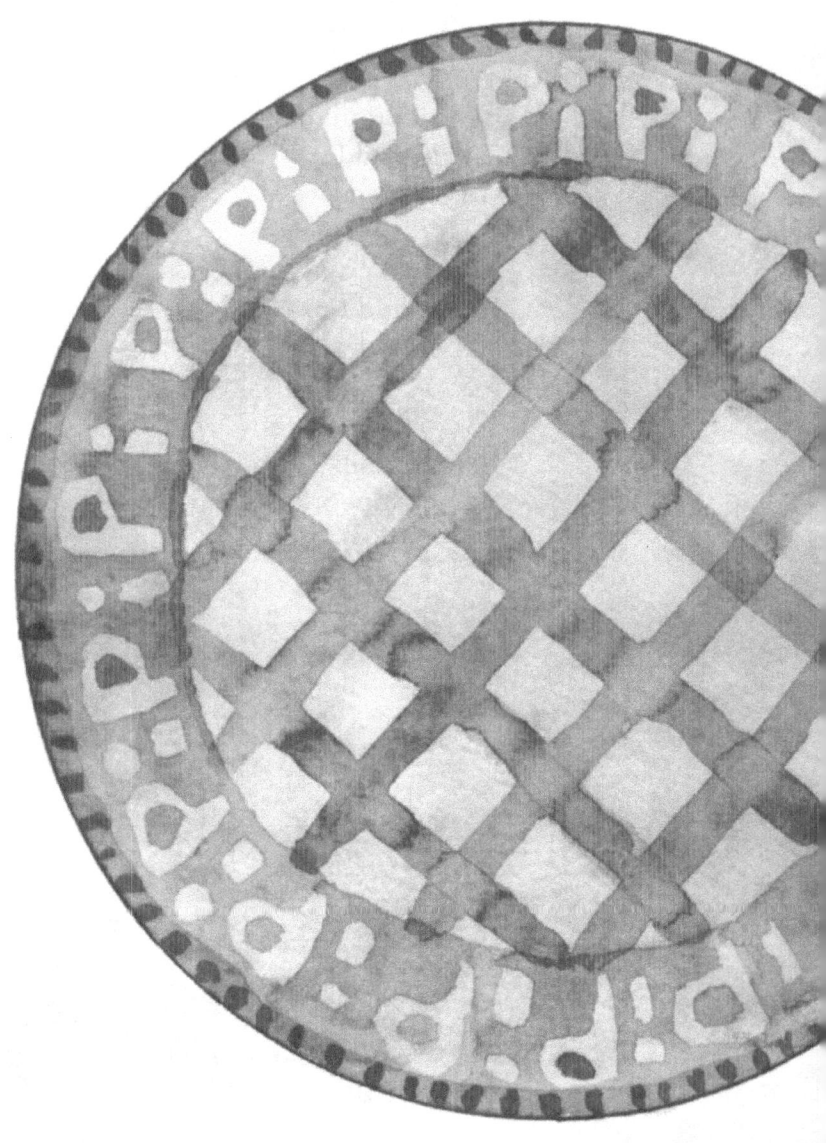

Anyone For Pi?

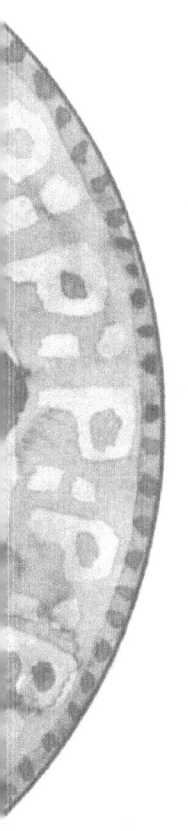

Pie in the sky.
Pie in the face.
Both bring a smile
to the human race.

But the pie that fills
with most wonder of all
is the pie they serve
at the mathematicians' ball

for their *pi* has no *e*
– it's no ordinary pastry –
and they sit in circles
of opulence

as they feast on diameter
and circumference.

'It's the ratio that matters,'
they conclude with a sigh
as they raise their glasses to *pi*.
'Come hell, come heaven,
let's propose a toast
to twenty-two over seven.'

A Parallel Meeting

On a day of unparalleled sunshine,
two strangers walk on parallel lines.
And parallel lines, they say, never meet.

But when sun pours down its honey-sweet
glow to make hearts glad for a summer,
two parallel 'hellos' find each other.

The Coming of the Hedrons

Tetrahedron
was a giant
with four equilateral faces,
so he stood out in a crowd
of folks with only one face.
Let's just say he was different,
until one day Tetrahedron
met a certain lady giant
named Octahedron
who had twice as many faces.
It was solid love at first sight,
for they had much in common.
They'd gaze at each other spellbound
and nuzzle faces with mighty sighs
and beautiful was the sound
of their names on each other's tongues.
O Tetrahedron
O Octahedron
Why don't we combine forms
to produce multiple hedrons?

And so a new generation
of multi-faced giants
began to walk the earth.

Hexahedron
of the six faces,
Dodecahedron
of the twelve faces,
Icosahedron
of the twenty faces.

How the folks with only one face
looked on in ancient wonder
at their geometric radiance.

Gone, gone are the dragons,
fallen to our weapons.
What's to be done with these hedrons?
Shall we approach them with a sword
or shall we join their cosmic dance?

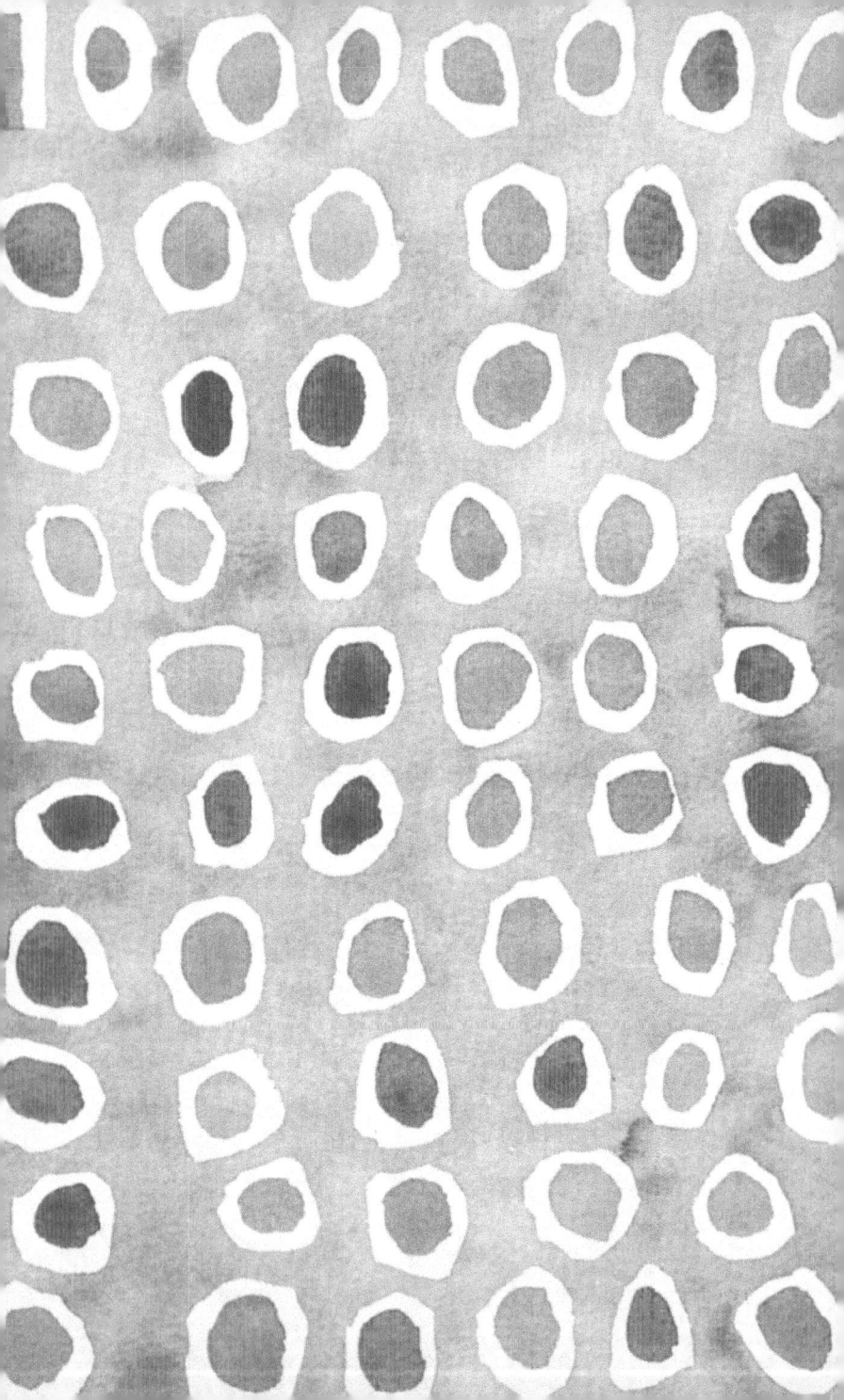

I am Googol

I am Googol
the goggle-eyed One,
leader of 100 zeros.

So gather your army
of trillions and quintillions.
I will outnumber their atoms.
For when I Googol
multiply myself
googol by googol,
let all the minds of East and West
be prepared to be googolplexed.

Not Half Scared

If a quarter moon
is one fourth of a full moon,

and if a fifth of a star
is one twinkling point,

and if I leave my door ajar
which is to say half-open
(or should that be half-closed?)
on a Halloween night,

and if half a pumpkin
comes creeping up the stairs
would I be a fraction scared?

Not half.

Sharing the Same Equation

Did Einstein, my namesake,
have a cat to sit on his lap
when he pondered gravitation?
No reason why a mathematician and a cat
can't share the same equation.

I wonder what his cat would make
of $E = mc^2$ and stuff like that?
Sure, a cat to a mathematician
is much more than a puss.
I'd say it was a plus,
for cats they say walk in straight lines
and are known to be passionately curious.
'And all I have,' said Einstein, 'is my curiosity.'

But I have my own theory.
Behind the whiskers of his moustache,
brainy Einstein was a cat in disguise
longing to ride on a beam of light
and paw at the laws of gravity.

HELLO H2O

When It's Freezing

When it's freezing
and my mouth
sends a trail of mist
into the air,
I know it's my lungs
releasing water vapour,
clouding up my glasses
by what's called condensation.

But I like to think
my mouth
is an Aladdin's lamp
and from my throat
a genie of smoke
is soaring.

Walking Pendulum

Mood swings.

Now I'm up.

Now I sing.

Now I'm glad.

Mood swings.

Now I'm down.

Now I sulk.

Now I'm glum.

Inertia	and	gravity
must be	turning	me
into a	walking	pendulum.

Hello H2O

Your body
is an ocean's body,
your skin
is a river's skin.

In your footsteps
the rain dances,
in your shadow
a lake sees itself.

With your echo
a waterfall speaks,
with your gestures
a fountain splashes itself.

You leave your signature
in puddles and leaks
– each a small reminder
that water was here.

Hello H_2O,
my two parts hydrogen,
one part oxygen friend
from my womb-swimming past.

My mouth will always be your glass.

My Humanoid Robot

My humanoid robot
has a brain that's powered
by a dual pentium
3 processor.

My humanoid robot
has gauges and sensors
all nicely built-in
to give it softer skin.

My humanoid robot
is an early riser,
no sleepyhead dosser,
and wakes me every morning.

My humanoid robot
helps to keep my room neat
and can easily beat
Dad at a game of Chess.

Still, Mum isn't impressed.
Whenever they compete,
she calls my humanoid robot
'a clever little cheat.'

Then my humanoid robot
flies off its pentium
and throws such a tantrum,
you'd swear it was human.

Blowing Bubbles

To you
I'm blowing bubbles.
To me
I'm conducting
an orchestra
of swirling light waves
and rainbow octaves.

To you
I'm blowing bubbles.
To me
I'm building
a nest
of planets
on a branch of breath.

It's Sad When A Kite's

forward motion
to the sky
becomes a backward
motion to the ground –
a colourful ruin
at your feet.

Your flying dragon
now fully earthbound.
Your singing bird
has lost its tongue.
Your dancing fish
collapsed in a heap.

What could have gone wrong?
Was gravity too strong?
Why did it lose its loop?
What made it go all droop

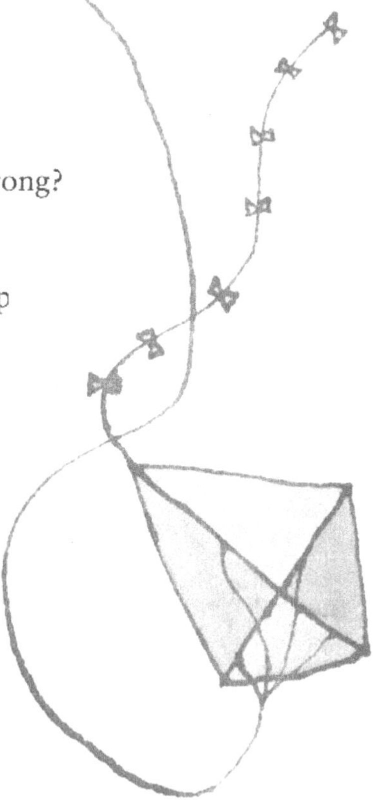

Was its forward motion
not enough to resist
the force of the wind?
Answer me, aerodynamics.

Two Of One

Little Bo Peep
has lost her cloned sheep
but she isn't
the least bit bothered,
for wherever one roams
there roams the other.
So she leaves them alone,
knowing they'll come home,
bringing each other's chromosomes.

But what would Little Bo Peep do,
if she were to meet
under a haycock fast asleep,
not one but two
of Little Boy Blue?
Each one an exact copy
of the other,
and each one just as lazy
as the other.

Neither blowing his horn
Neither blowing his horn

No thought
for the sheep in the meadow
No thought
for the cow in the corn.

A Watt?

You ask me
what's a watt?
Better ask Mr. Watt.
He'll tell you what's what
on the subject of watts.
He comes from a long line of Watts.
All I know
is that a watt's
got something
to do with a lightbulb's glow.
That's what,
or whatever.

What would a bald man
want with a comb?
When I rub this comb
along the atomic
particles
of my shiny
egg of a head,
and the teeth tickle
my knackered
follicles,
I remind myself
how once my hair
was elastic.
And believe you me,
my skull begins to glow
with the mere memory
of static.

It's Shining Watermelons

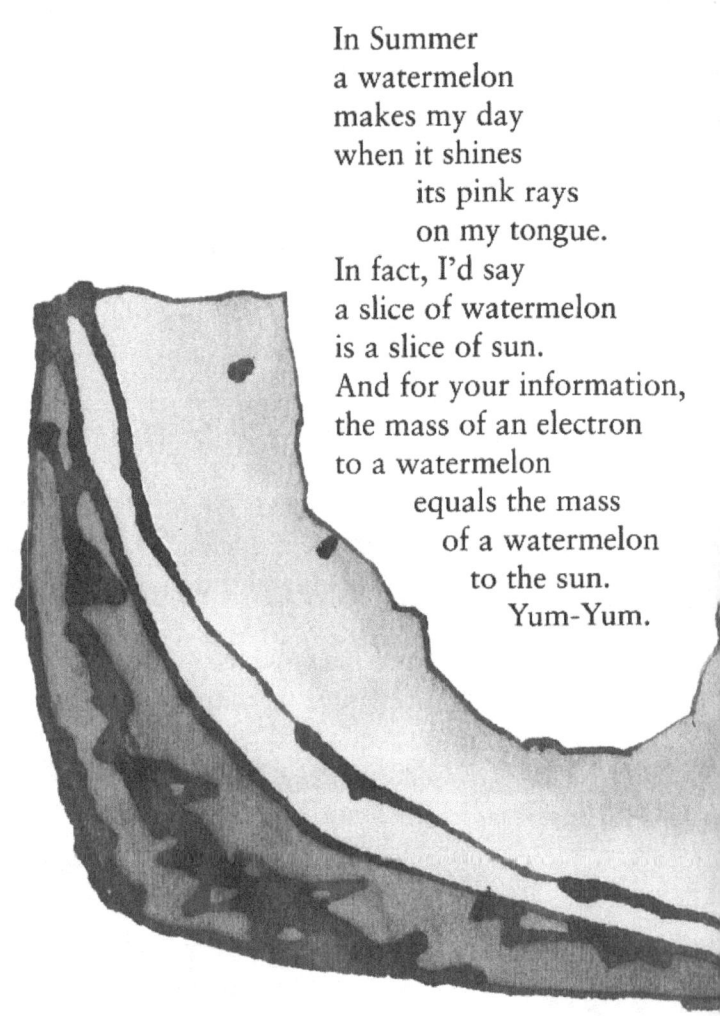

In Summer
a watermelon
makes my day
when it shines
      its pink rays
      on my tongue.
In fact, I'd say
a slice of watermelon
is a slice of sun.
And for your information,
the mass of an electron
to a watermelon
      equals the mass
        of a watermelon
        to the sun.
          Yum-Yum.

RecipeForAFloatingChineseCompass

Take a thin leaf of iron.
Marinate with a lodestone.
Flatten into shape of fish.
Heat until red hot.
Remove from fire with tongs.
Float in a bowl of seawater.
Head of fish will point south.
Tail of fish will point true north.
Say long live magnetised needle.

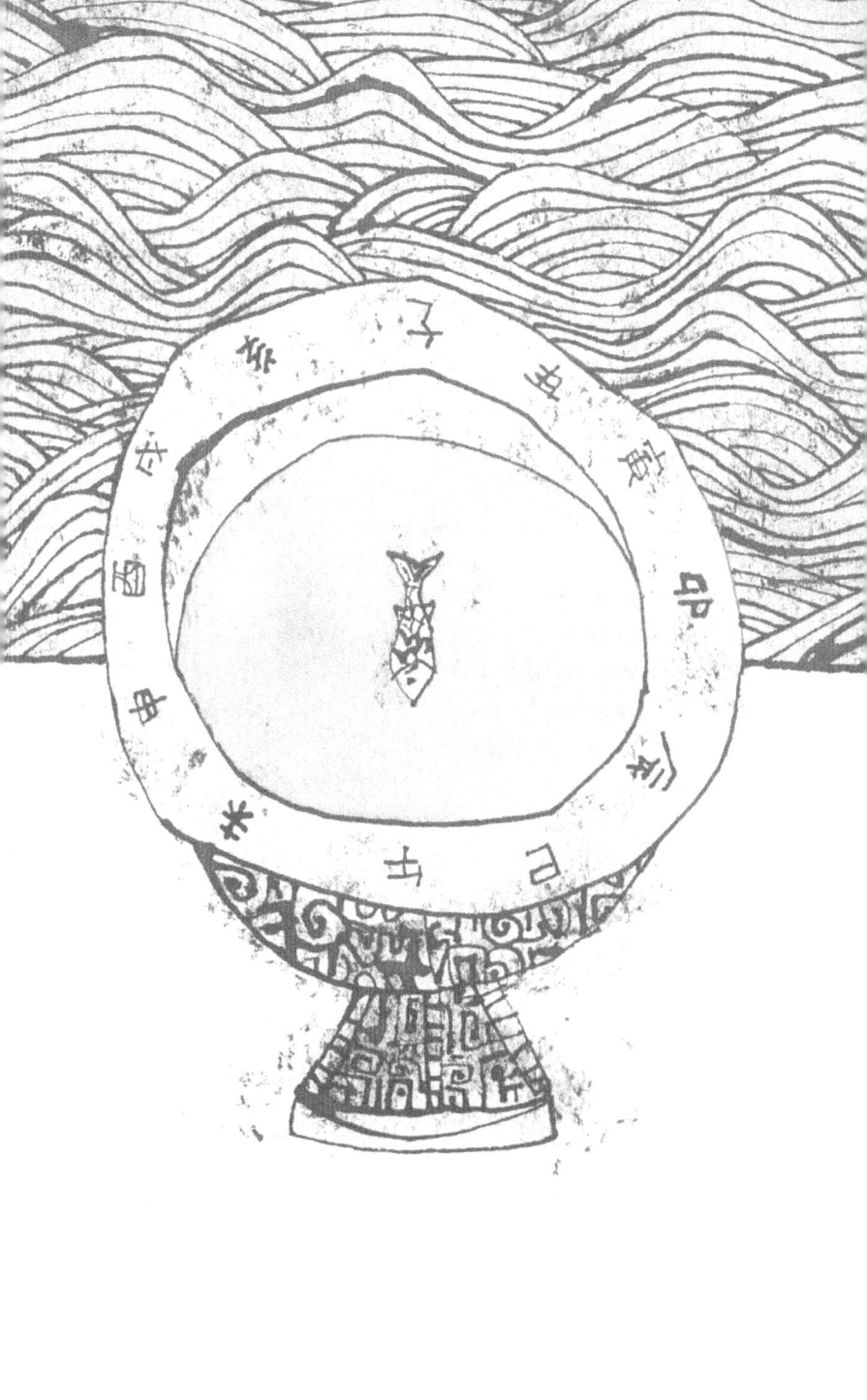

Clockwise

I'm your bedside mate.
And I'll let you all
into a secret.
If my quartz crystal
didn't oscillate
to tune my pulse rate
to ticking tempo,
you'll surely be late.

But I say nothing.
Just sit in my place
as squat as a toad
and keep a straight face,
pointing to time's road.
Tomorrow at dawn,
I'm set to alarm.
May your dreams be deep
when I steal your sleep.

Melting Point

'Why are you crying?'
the little girl asked the giant.

'Because solids melt
at a certain temperature,'
the giant replied.

The little girl nodded, 'that's right.
Plutonium, for example, has a melting point
of 1184 degrees Fahrenheit.'

The giant sighed and said, 'you're very bright.
And it seems I've just met my melting point.'

With that, the giant cried
himself into a fountain.

Speculating About Specs

'Let us give thanks
for convex lenses,'
said the long-sighted.

'Let us give thanks
for concave lenses,'
said the short-sighted.

'Let us give thanks
for noses,' said the clown.
'Of course, I'm delighted

with my new pair of specs.
But if noses didn't exist,
how would we balance these discs?'

99

A Few Questions
For The Tooth Fairy

I have a few questions
for the tooth fairy.
Now, don't get me wrong,
I certainly welcome
waking to a coin
under my pillow.
But I need to know
the truth, the whole truth
and nothing but the truth.
What would a fairy want
with a once wobbly tooth?
Does she recycle it?
Can it be that tooth fairies
eat too may sweets?
Do they get rotten teeth?

Do they have cavities
that need to be filled?
Have they their own kind
of dental drill
and ultra-sound probe
to help them fight plaque?
Is there fluoride
in fairy drinking water
or do they just fly off
to calcium-rich flowery places?
These are a few of the questions
I'm dying to ask.
And I'd do anything
to see a tooth fairy
smiling with braces.

Five Reasons Why I Would Volunteer For Outer Space

1. It would be good to live in a weightless neighbourhood.

2. I could do my homework while turning somersaults.

3. It would be fun
   to watch my spoon
   fly away
   from my Cocoa Pops.

4. I could boast
   I've actually been
   to the loo
   on the moon.

5. If I'm late
   I could say
   'My alarm clock, Miss,
   Just floated off.'

The Day The Metals Marched

Out of the earth's crust they come.
Out of the furnace they come
after centuries of combustion.
From every direction they come
and they need no drum –
these molten messengers
marching, marching to the sound
of their own names:

Aurum
Argentum
Cuprum
Ferrum
Staunum

All taking up position.
All ready to stand as one,
despite their different forms
of lumps, blades, jewels, wires, rods.
All in blinding splendour.
Iron and Bronze rubbing shoulders.
Gold and Silver mingling rays.
Copper glinting next to Tin –

And on the day the metals marched
Plumbum just couldn't wait to join in.
Yes, old Plumbum, better known as Lead,
though grey of hair and slow of foot,
fell in line with –

> Aurum
> Argentum
> Cuprum
> Ferrum
> Staunum

Meanwhile, the humans stayed indoors.

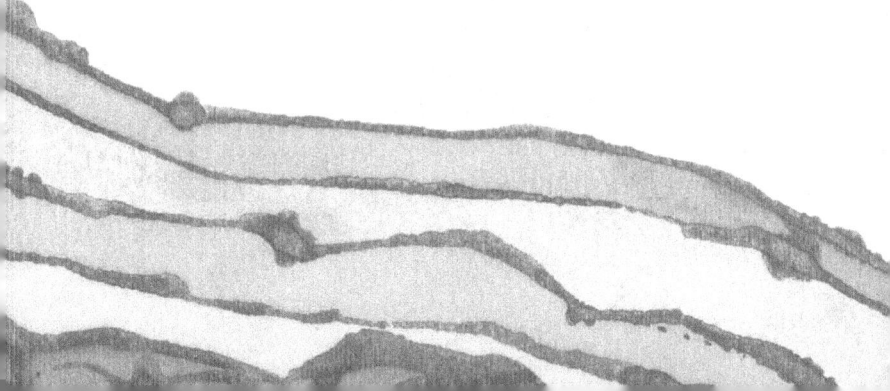

Gifts For Earth's Atmosphere

By sea, by land, by air
they came bearing gifts
to Earth's atmosphere.

Nitrogen and Oxygen
were most generous
with their own gases.
And Argon and Carbon Dioxide
also took pride
in giving themselves.

And water brought vapour
and crystals of ice,
and the ocean thought
a bouquet of salt
would be nice,
and the flowers
not to be outdone,
presented their pollen
in wind-wrapped particles.

And from every direction,
Earth's atmosphere
received a shower of gifts
– including a sad windfall
of ashes and soot
and gases that pollute.

Atmospheric Traveller

Of course, I've braved
the six layers
of the atmosphere.
You name it, I've been there.

From the dense Troposphere
to the less dense Stratosphere,
through a chemical buzz
of the Mesosphere,
past the plasma
of the Ionosphere,
rising higher
to the raging Thermosphere,
till I came at last
to the Exosphere,
where weird gases
made me welcome.

But I'd rather
settle down here
among common
stones and grasses.
Other spheres
are not for me,
I feel safer
with gravity.

Pigeon's Flying Tips

'It's all to do with lift and thrust,'
said the pigeon to the pilot.
'I lift my wings at take-off time.
And in the wind I place my trust.
By the way, my propeller
never needs to be replaced.
And all the sky's my airspace.'

Leonardo da Vinci's Notebooks

To Leonardo da Vinci,
a bird in flight
was an aerodynamic delight.

What better way to learn
about aerial locomotion
than from creatures born for aviation?

So he studied birds, sketched birds –
their lift, their glide, their wing movements.
He even studied wind currents.

Then he turned his thoughts
from the miracle of feathers
to ordinary things like propellers.

And four hundred years or more,
before a helicopter was seen,
he designed a flying machine.

They called it Ornithopter,
a funny sort of word
that comes from the Greek for bird.

This isn't surprising.
And he must have had fun jotting down
forward ideas in backwards handwriting.

Strictly Speaking

Strictly speaking, they say
the moon doesn't shine
since it has no light
of its own.
Strictly speaking, they say
the moon's glow
is a sun-loan.

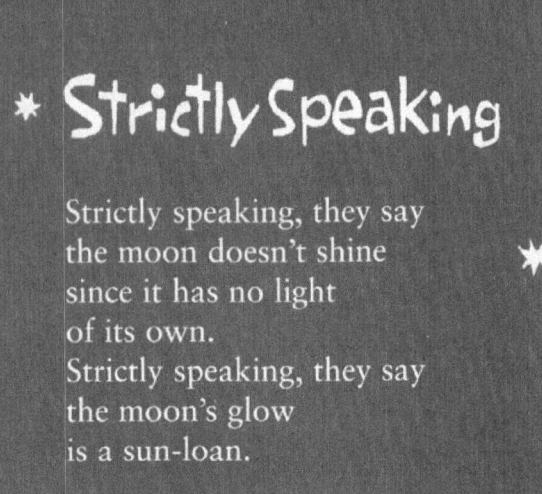

But on a full-moon night
when stars flock that yellow,
it's no business of mine
if the moon does borrow
the sun's light.
When it's dark
I borrow from the moon.

Daydreaming Galileo

'Daydreaming again, Galileo?'
his teacher asked with a frown.
'Aren't you supposed to be reading?'

'I am,' replied Galileo.
'Don't you see my eyes turning
the pages of the skies?

I'm busy browsing
the grand book of the universe.
A book I simply can't put down.'

Under Galileo's Glass

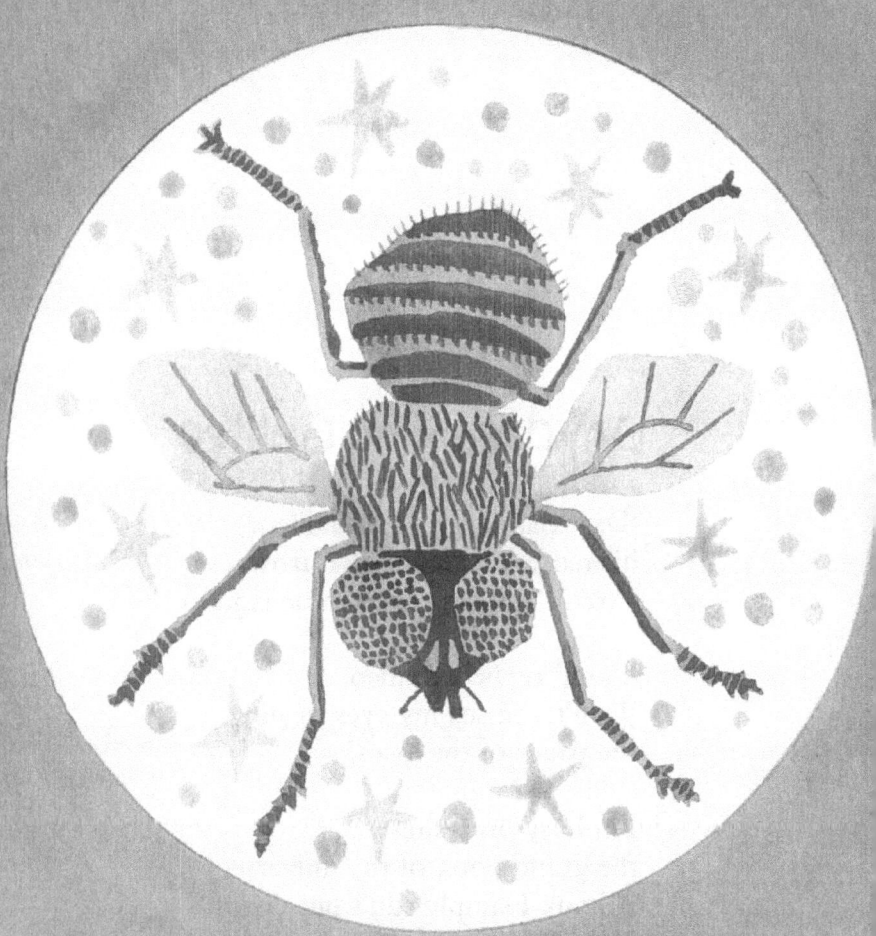

A tiny gnat
shows off its godliness.

A grey moth
becomes a galaxy.

An upside down fly
puts on the wings of a star.

And is that a horrible
bloodsucking flea

treating the eye
to a small constellation?

All this is possible
under Galileo's glass.

Even the smallest
of creepy-crawlies

dares you to guess
its wriggling zodiac.

One Family?

If I am made
of atoms and molecules,
and you are made
of atoms and molecules,
and all the world is made
of atoms and molecules,
does this mean the human race
belongs to one family
of atoms and molecules?
Then why aren't we as together
as tadpoles in a pool?
They never teach you this
in science at school.

Weighty Thoughts

Isn't it great,
thought the astronaut,
to be free
of gravity –
a dangling bait
in a weightless sea.

One thing bothers me,
thought the astronaut.
If my spaceship lands
at heaven's gate,
will my earthly words
still bear weight?

And Then The Sun Spoke

Take all the fuel
known to planet earth.

Burn your wood, your coal,
get your oil roaring.

The energy soaring
from your humble fires

will be nowhere near
a billionth –

Yes, a billionth
of the heat and light

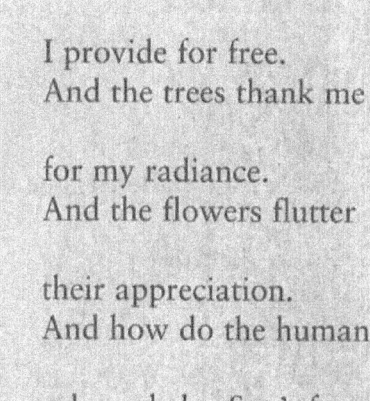

I provide for free.
And the trees thank me

for my radiance.
And the flowers flutter

their appreciation.
And how do the humans

acknowledge Sun's favours?
Believe it or not –

By sunshades and sunblock.

DNA(1)

It's easier
to say
DNA –
that's no tongue twister.

But somehow
I feel a whizz kid
when I say
DEOXYRIBONUCLEIC ACID

especially
with my mouth full.

DNA(2)

Adenine: Guanine
Cytosine: Thymine.
They come in pairs
and they're all yours,
all mine.

Building blocks we share
with living things.
Whether curled
within a nucleus
or floating free,
they make us us,
unique you,
unique me.

DNA(3)

If I climb
the ladder
of my DNA
would I lose my way
among the cells
of my body?

Would it be okay to step on
those chemical rungs
and balance
on spiralling pairs
of nitrogen bases?
What awaits
among those sugars
and phosphates?

Would they lead me
to magic places
and marvels of mind
or would I find
myself
face to face
with skeletons
in a cupboard?

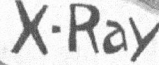

X·Ray

Call me X-ray.

X-ray will do.

I see through you.

Whether your skin

be black, white,

yellow or blue.

An inside view

is what I get.

That's a fact, mate.

I offer you

your skeleton

served on a photographic

plate.

The Wind Sets The Record Right

'It's not electricity
making those telephone wires hum.

It's my velocity.
Yes, it's me, it's me,' said the wind.

'It's the plectrum
of my breath
as I strum
those telephone wires
for my guitar.

I the wind
serenading
a star.'

Cloud Chant

You call us
names like 'ominous'
but we call our grey 'glorious'

I thundery Cumulonimbus
I showery Nimbostratus
I crystally Cirrostratus
I drizzly Stratocumulus
I icy Cirrocumulus
I watery Altocumulus

Feathery we may be
Foggy we may be
Woolly we may be
Wispy we may be

But grand is our status –
we grand descendants
of Cumulus, Cirrus and Stratus.

Photosynthesis

When sunlight dances
on the tips
of leaves

and plants for joy
open their lips
to drink it in

and the breeze
makes a violin
of every tree

and even weeds
one by one
cry out for a kiss

of light and carbon –
a sheer spree of green.
Is this what they mean

by photosynthesis?

Consider The Peanut

Consider the peanut,
this humble jewel
housed in a shell.
Consider the peanut,
this small traveller
across continents
with many secrets to tell.

Consider the peanut,
and consider
George Washington Carver
and his peanut experiments.
From peanuts and their skins and shells,
he brought forth diesel fuel,
writing ink, newsprint paper,
not to mention face ointments,
toilet soap, toothpaste, shampoo,
even shoe polish,
and of course peanut dainties
like brownies and caramel.

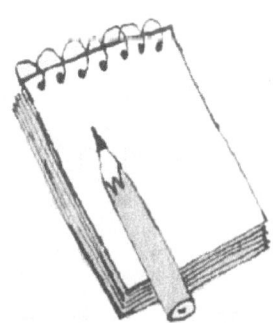

Consider the peanut,
and consider
this plant doctor
who learnt to read, write and spell,
even as he saw his parents wake
to slavery's bell
and heard the music of the blues.
He would make the peanut story
his life's study
for his 'cookstove chemistry.'
Yes, he would spread the good news
of the unsung peanut –

this winged bean
that ripens underground,
this lifeline vine
for forest-dwellers,
this decoration
on an Inca pot,
this discovery
in an Egyptian tomb,
and in years to come –
this astronaut's gift
from planet earth to moon.

We, The Noble Gases

We, the noble gases,
are the upper classes
of the atmosphere.
When we throw a party,
it's a very private affair.
Strictly by invitation
and liquid distillation.
We don't easily mix, we six.

Can Lord and Lady Argon,
Krypton, Neon, Xenon, Radon,
not to mention
His Highness Helium,
rub shoulders with the common?
We, the noble gases,
maintain our noble station
in noble isolation.

The Dead Sea Speaks

Freshwater streams may feed me,
yet salt is my destiny
and brine my very being.

People talk a lot
about my deadly salinity,
my density, my whatnot.

But from the depths of my valleybed
across the burning desert sands,
let these words of mine flow red.

Dead Sea I am in name, but not in deed,
for underneath my salty shroud
countless living microbes do me proud.

Superbugs' Chorus

Superbugs, that's us, anonymous.
Germs. Microbes. Bacillus.
Come on folks, what's all the fuss?
Join the bacteria chorus.
We invisible hordes
colonise your chopping boards,
squat upon your rugs,
reside within your hair,
lay down roots everywhere,
for we are superbugs.
Send in the penicillin.
Bring on the ampicillin.

We'll have a lie-in in your skin.
So consider yourself immune
all smug in your germ-free cocoon?
We'll catch you and catch you soon.
You there in your squeaky-clean zone,
we're nesting in your mobile phone.
Yet we superbugs are rays of hope,
we bring life to your microscope.
So why not give decay a chance
and share the planet with our kind?
We are the children of your waste,
the offspring of your extravagance,
and while humans dine and die,
we superbugs dance, we dance.

Who'll Save Dying Man?

Who'll save dying Man?
  I, said the Baboon.
Transplant my bone marrow,
and he'll wake tomorrow.

Who'll save dying Man?
  I, said the Chimpanzee.
He's welcome to my brain,
for deep down we're the same.

Who'll save dying Man?
  I, said the Pig.
I'll give him my liver.
May he live forever.

Who'll save dying Man?
  I, said the Sheep.
Let him have my kidney,
and that would be for free.

Who'll save dying Man?
  I, said Rat.
My retina would do
to make his vision new.

Who'll save dying Man?
  I, said Squid.
He can have our nerve cells,
for sea-folk wish him well.

Who'll save dying Man?
  I, said the Physician.
I'll save him with my skills,
though dying Man once killed.

Thanks for the offer,
  said dying Man.
But I'd like to request
a Dodo for a doner.

And the animals fell
a-whispering secretly:
  O dying Man
has lost his memory.

Radium And Madame Curie

The birds didn't sing,
the bees didn't hum,
when Marie Curie
discovered Radium.

But the atoms danced
their secret dance,
happy to release
their energy.

Marie had worked for years
with her husband Pierre,
and to the Curies,
physics was their chemistry.

Marie would leave her bed
for her drafty shed,
drawn to the mystery
of a new element.

She had to explore
this unnamed continent –
map out the rays
that turned air to glow-worms.

And with no protective clothing,
she dared to greet Radium
– great healer
– great destroyer.

That's why the birds didn't sing
and the bees didn't hum.
But the nuclear atoms
danced to their own drum.

In Praise of The Eraser

I would not chew
on the delete key
of the computer
if I were you.

So sing in praise
of the eraser,
your little chewy
vulcanised buddy.

Someone once said,
'any fool can write.
It takes a genius
to erase.'

Now at my PC
lost in thought's deep mist,
I must say I miss
an eraser's kiss.

To erase is bliss.

Electro·Magnetic Haunting

Since an electro-magnetic wave passes
through solids, liquids and gases
and invisibly enters a room,

it would be great to come back from the grave
as an electro-magnetic wave.
On Halloween night, I'd haunt a vacuum.

Quivers In The Life Of A Quark

1.
A Quark
can neither
quack not bark

for a Quark
is neither
duck nor dog

though perhaps
a bit of both.
A Quark

likes to swim
in a cosmic tub
as it wags

its tail
in the sub-
atomic

dark.

2.
An atom called Quark
met an atom called Anti-Quark.

But neither knew
what the other was called,
and it didn't matter.
A Quark to a Quark was a Quark,
whether red, green or blue.

Without any fuss,
Quark and Anti-Quark
quivered their particles
on a cosmic ray.

And to this day
Quark and Anti-Quark
live in a nucleus

And their sub-atomic marriage
remains a mystery to us.

Footsteps In My Lab

In an ancient time
deep in a forest's mists,
Indian grandma walked her journey,
and the trees and plants
were her friends
as well as her chemists.
From birch she made tea
and no-one mentioned Vitamin C,
and chokecherry berries
were not labelled cough syrup,
and no-one mentioned pick-me-up.

In an ancient time
deep in a forest's mists,
Indian grandma walked her journey,
and to ease the back pains
she would not let win,
she puffed her pipe at peace
and breathed the willow in.

And no-one mentioned aspirin,
and the cottonwood leaves
were her godsent plaster,
and balsam bark would cool a bruise.

In an ancient time
deep in a forest's mists,
Indian grandma walked her journey,
and to stop a fever
beating its sweating drum
on a grandchild's brow,
she would ask the help
of wild geranium.
And raspberry was ready
for a runny tummy,
and no-one mentioned prescription.

Indian grandma, long gone to rest.
Your medicine bag
still haunts my medicine chest.
I hear your footsteps in my lab.

THE RAINMAKER DANCED

When Questions Are Bliss

If I lie
on a page
am I a free word?

If I fly
in a cage
am I a trapped bird?

If I cry
with eyes of green
am I a weeping leaf?

Answers are folly
when questions are bliss
Without questions, do I exist?

Rooms

In the keeping room
we keep many things.
Exactly what, I'm not telling you.

In the sleeping room
naturally we sleep
and hope for a dream, perhaps two.

In the peeping room
we take a peep at life
while life peeps back out of the blue.

In the leaping room
we like to leap about.
It's known as doing the kangaroo.

In the heaping room
we heap our junk and stuff
for recycling into newer than new.

In the weeping room
we weep our hearts out
till the past has received its due.

That's when we return
to the keeping room
and keep our thoughts to ourselves.

The Rainmaker Danced

The rainmaker danced
the rainmaker danced
the rainmaker danced
and down came
the rains
in a flash.

'Bad news,' says the umpire.
'That's washed out the cricket match.'

Still the rainmaker danced
the rainmaker danced
the rainmaker danced
and the sky
surrendered its blue
to grey and more grey.

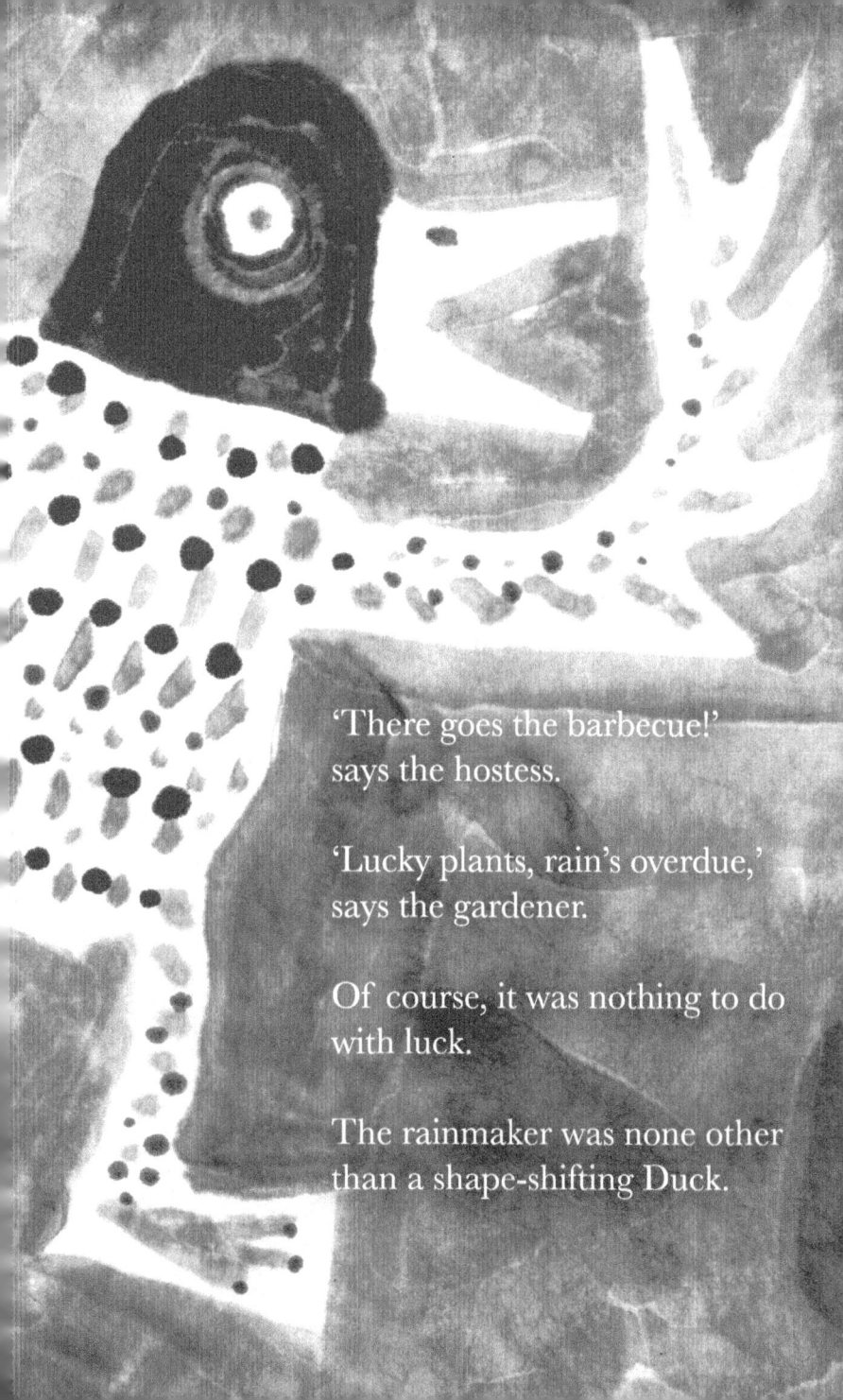

'There goes the barbecue!'
says the hostess.

'Lucky plants, rain's overdue,'
says the gardener.

Of course, it was nothing to do
with luck.

The rainmaker was none other
than a shape-shifting Duck.

The Dew–Stealers

Who'd want to steal dew?
Maybe not me, maybe not you?
Then again, if you'd discovered
that dewdrops were heaven's pearls

(the precious spittle of the stars
according to that Roman Pliny)
yes, if dew meant liquid revenue
then even me, even you

might be tempted before sunrise
to creep up on unsuspecting grass
and steal from its store of gems
praying we're not caught on CCTV

sneaking off with dawn's treasury
still melting from our fingertips.

Hello Moon Hello Pig

Moon decided one night
to make a pig of herself.

So Moon shrugged off her bright yellow hood
and without saying goodbye to the stars
made her soundless way down sky's staircase
slipping into the first puddle's embrace.

It was hard work learning to drool and slobber
but Moon soon got the hang of rolling over
sidewards and bellywards in good old mud
until wallowing was easy as waxing and waning.

With more time and more practice
Moon got used to this form of mucky bathing.
In fact it became Moon's secret habit.
Surprise surprise she soon has herself a litter

of little potbellied curly-tailed moonlings.
And guess what? Moon showed her joy by grunting.

On The Run From Colours

Green misled me into the woods.
Blue tried to drown me in the sea.

White smothered me in balls of clouds.
Yellow caught me on a double yellow line.

Red greeted me with hands of blood.
Brown imprisoned my steps in clay.

Black offered to close my eyes in sleep.
But a nightmare got in the way.

Now even grey looks out to get me.
Fog, what are you? Friend or enemy?

The Girl Who Married An Iron Stove

'Father, Father, O what have I done?
I've promised to marry an old iron stove
that helped me find my way out of the woods.'

'Daughter Daughter, I think I smell enchantment
when wedding bells are what make a stove content.
Go ask your mother for her humble opinion.'

'Don't worry, my child,' her mother declared.
'I'll see thee wed before I see my grave.
Shame it's an iron stove (not a microwave)!'

'But frogs have been kissed into princely hubbies.
Who knows what's to be of your bridegroom stove?
The strangest things happen in the name of love.'

'Your mother has spoken wisely,' the father agreed.
'A stove for a son-in-law will keep the neighbours guessing.
And a little stove for a grandchild will be our blessing.'

'Yes, we'll be the envy of the neighbourhood,'
nodded his wife. 'For when the winter takes its toll,
we shall have little grand stoves to warm our bones.'

The bride-to-be said not a word, simply smiled
as she scrubbed that stove with brush and with knife
until she heard a wee voice inside that iron prison

whispering: 'She who sets me free shall be my wife.
She who restores to me the lost light of day.
For I am not one formed of iron, but of clay.'

The Naming of Giants

A giant's name
should bludgeon the tongue
with a thundering sound –
a mouthful of syllables
to be savoured and gobbled.

Far better to be known as
a humungous blunderer
with a name like Blunderbore
or Blockerknob or Gogamog
than plain old Bill or Bob.

So says I, Gozzlemorebum the Gozzler,
son of Sizzlemorebum the Sizzler,
we whose ancient knuckles carved out hills
before the coming of peeny-puny mortals
with simpleton names like Jack and Jill.

Of Course I Believe In

Of course I believe in
Extra-terrestrials with
                extendable mandibles
the Yeti's mega footprint
                whose owner is untraceable
Nessie the monster who makes
                of a lake a habitable temple
Not to mention
the unicorn's singular
horn. Believe me, that was no fable.

It's not that I'm gullible
or even impressionable.
It's just that I respect the cred
                in incredible.

Seeking Answers

Do triangles
   ever get into a tangle
      when their sides meet their angles?

That fellow Pythagoras
   was he by any chance
      a pie enthusiast?

And is the Isosceles
   a rare form of eye disease?
      Someone answer please.

Though these questions of mine
   are mathematically pitched,
I'd say they'd be better answered
   by a patient psychiatrist.

Yu and Hi

And now beside Yellow River,
not far from shade of bamboo,
sits Chinese Empreror, Yu,
stroking chin as he ponders
mighty possible flood water.
'A dam!' thinks Emperor Yu
(who is also engineer).

As he wonders where to turn,
a voice says out of blue.
'Look on my back and learn.'
Who should this be but Turtle.
Not just any turtle, mind you.
But wise old black turtle named Hi,
ambassador of earth and sky.

Says divine Turtle to Emperor:
'As you are Yu and I am Hi,
I can see you are troubled
by thoughts of rising water.
But the dark markings of my shell
shall lighten your despair.
See the nine numbers on my back?
Therein lies a magic square.'

So by light of day, by lamp of night,
Emperor Yu studies those numbers all.
Adds them right to left, adds them left to right.
Adds them vertical, adds them horizontal.
Yes, Yu even adds them diagonal.
Yet answer, same, same. Always fifteen.
Why fifteen? What can this fifteen mean?

At long last, after much loss of sleep,
inspired Emperor Yu declares,
'Turtle's back shall be my maths teacher.
The dams and canals for my people
shall be laid like Turtle's magic square.
But to Yellow River, ever rising,
we must make fifteen offerings.'

Seagull Chant

Against a ship's
bulk of hull
Seagull Seagull
you dare your own
feathered hull
screech-beak-full
screech-beak-full.

Through storm and lull
by moon-pull
by sun-pull
Seagull Seagull
with you still around
the sea's never dull
the sea's never dull.

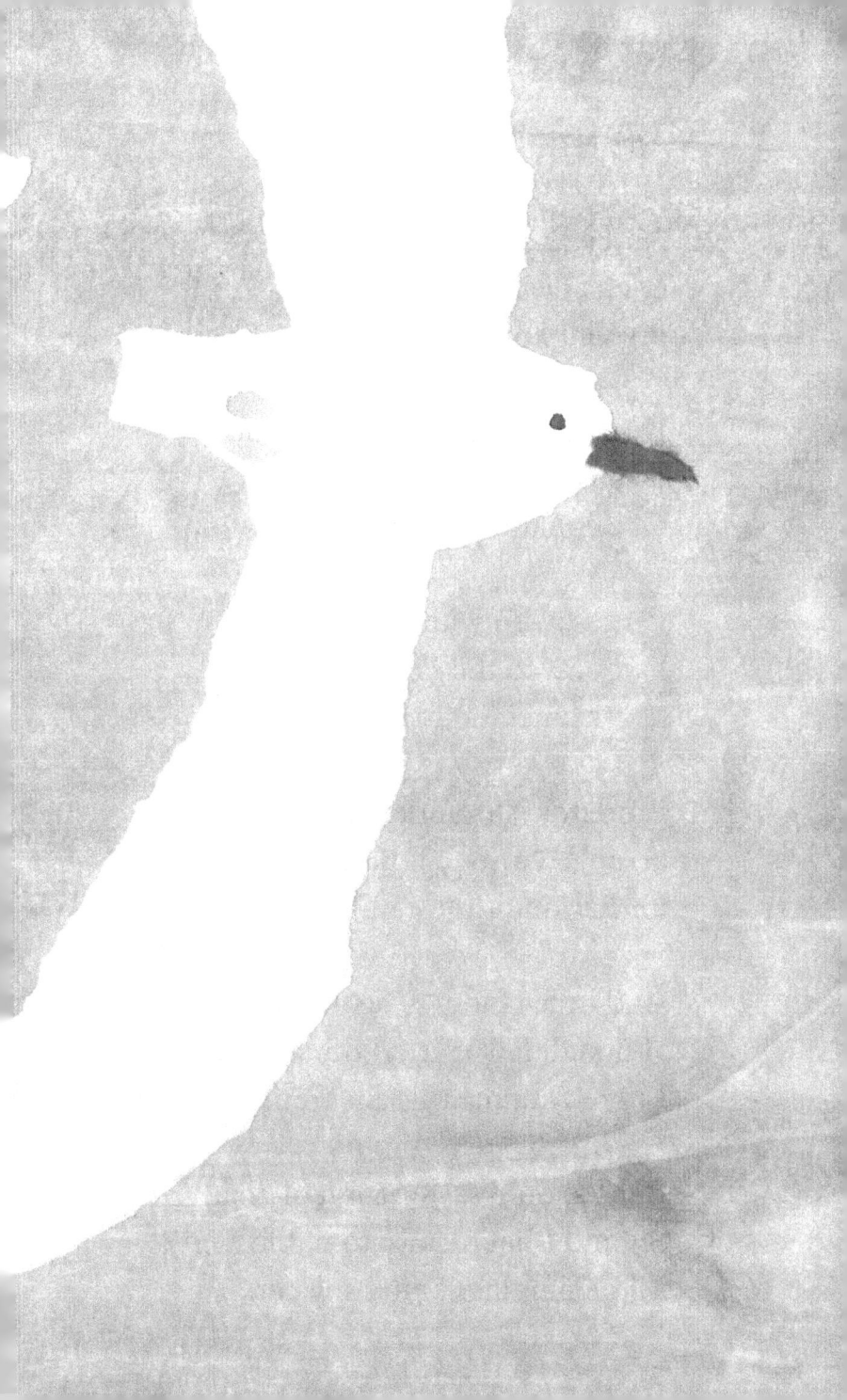

The Naming of a City

Ah Peritas, my Peritas,
cried Alexander the Great,
grieving for his faithful dog. Gone alas!

Peritas, who'd stood at his side
through battle thick and thin
of elephants and javelins.

Peritas, who with bark and bite
had braved the Persian cavalry,
never flinching from a fight.

Emperor Alexander, all tearful,
arranged a state funeral
for his long-time canine companion.

And in his sadness he declared:
'Though it is true all things come to pass,
I hereby name this city Peritas.'

But I should say enough of that.
Should I have cause to name a city,
I'll be naming it after my cat.

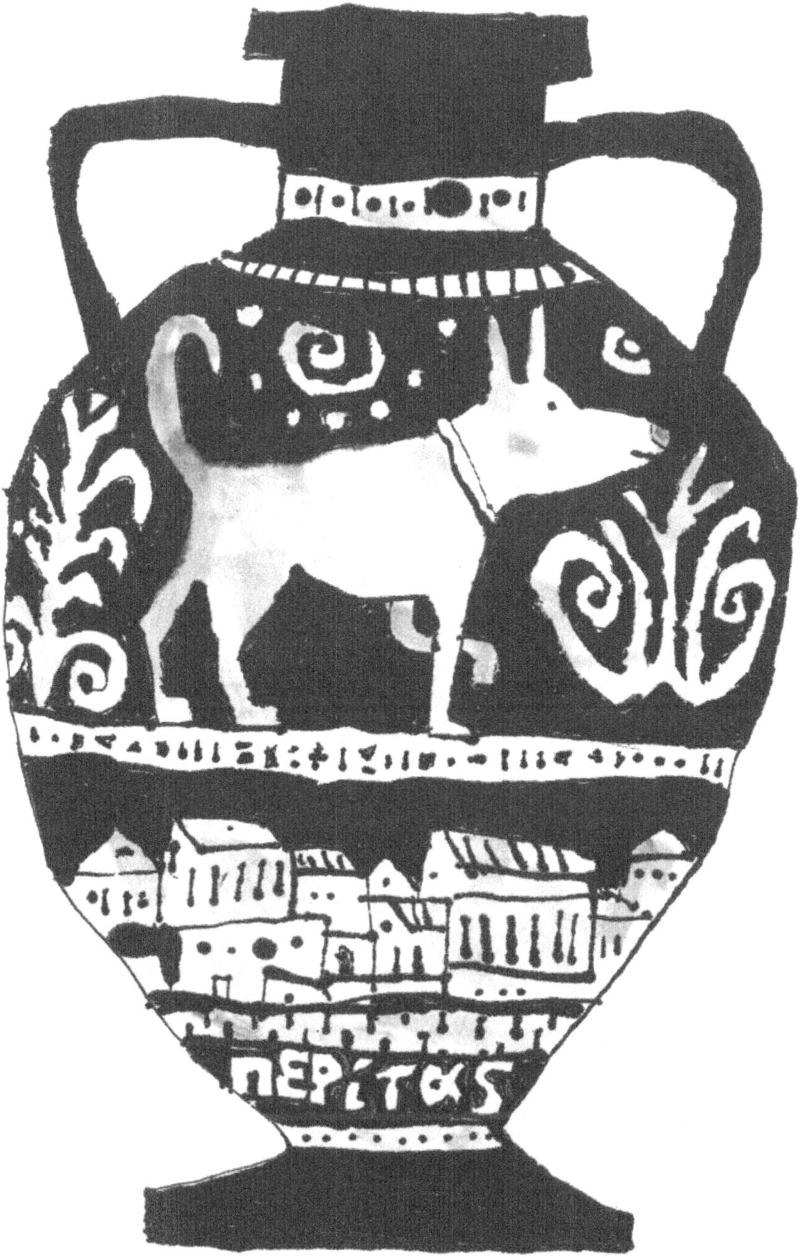
ΠΕΡίΤαS

Saluting Laika, the Sputnik Dog

Best first to launch a four-footer
into extra-terrestrial space
than to risk a two-footer
from what's known as the human race.

So up goes a husky mongrel
by the name of Laika.
But a capsule is no kennel
and soon Laika is a goner.

Alas, for Man's so-called best friend,
the end was Greekly tragic.
Laika snuffed it in a sputnik
with little time for last requests.

Near Moscow, Laika's monument
now rests for nation and for flag.
A canine cosmonauth and heroine
whose tail once knew how to wag.

The Countdown To Mars

'Mars, here I come,' said the scientist,
who was first among the chosen few.
'What old Galileo glimpsed was just a clue.
Landing on Mars, now that's a breakthrough!'

'Not a trip to be missed,' said the historian.
'To think an advanced civilisation might exist on Mars!
Wow! Fills me with mind boggling bliss!
I've lived my life for a moment like this.'

'Wouldn't miss Mars for the world,' said the surgeon.
And there sitting space-suited in the capsule
was one known far and wide as simply Fool.
How did he find himself in this gathering?

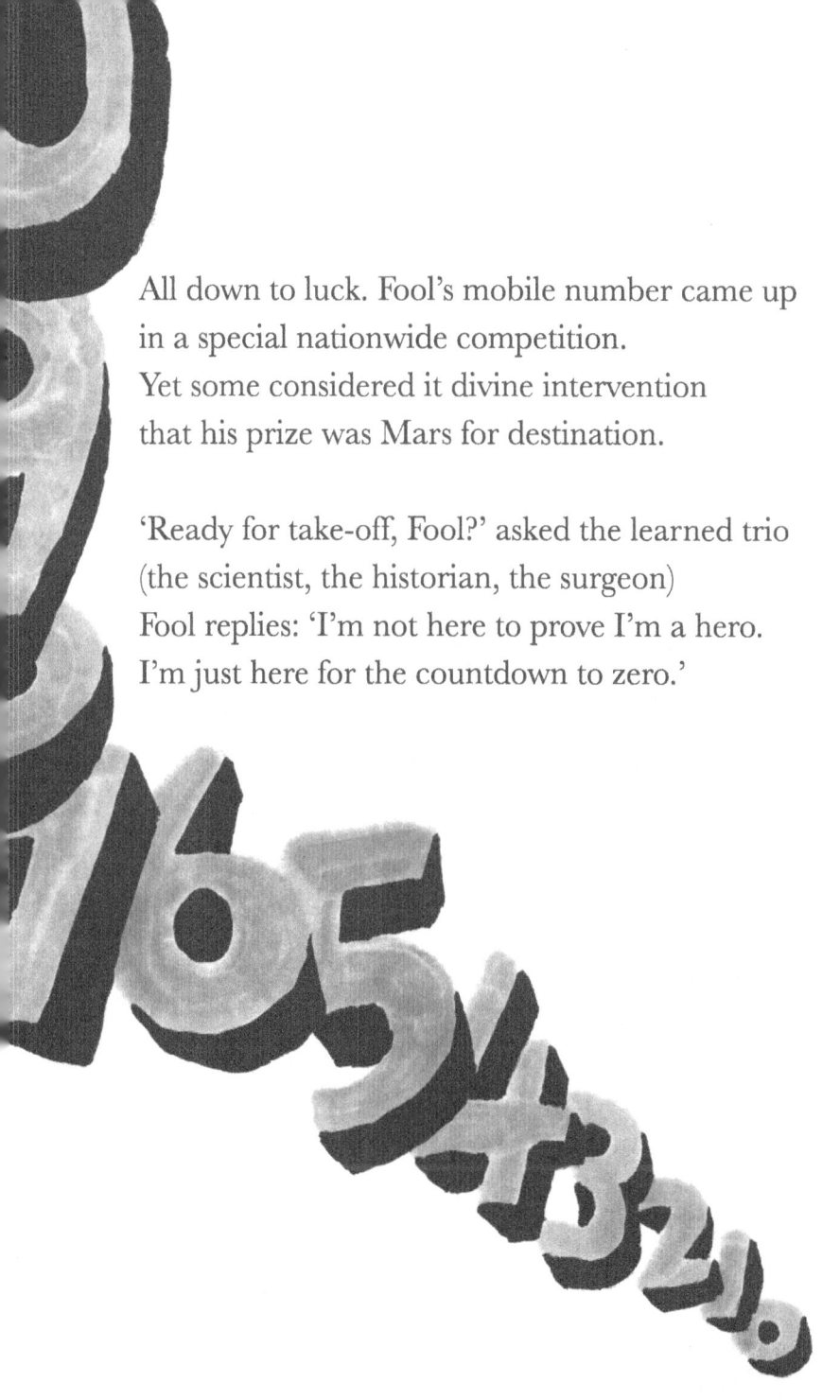

All down to luck. Fool's mobile number came up
in a special nationwide competition.
Yet some considered it divine intervention
that his prize was Mars for destination.

'Ready for take-off, Fool?' asked the learned trio
(the scientist, the historian, the surgeon)
Fool replies: 'I'm not here to prove I'm a hero.
I'm just here for the countdown to zero.'

GOVERNMENT WARNING!

YOU ARE ENTERING
A TICKLE-FREE ZONE.
ANY FUNNY BUSINESS
WITH THE FUNNY BONE
IS AGAINST THE LAW.
A TICKLE-INDUCED HA HA
OR UNAUTHORISED GUFFAW
IS STRICTLY FORBIDDEN
UNLESS BY WRITTEN AGREEMENT
BETWEEN THE TICKLER AND THE TICKLISH.
LAUGH AT YOUR OWN RISK.

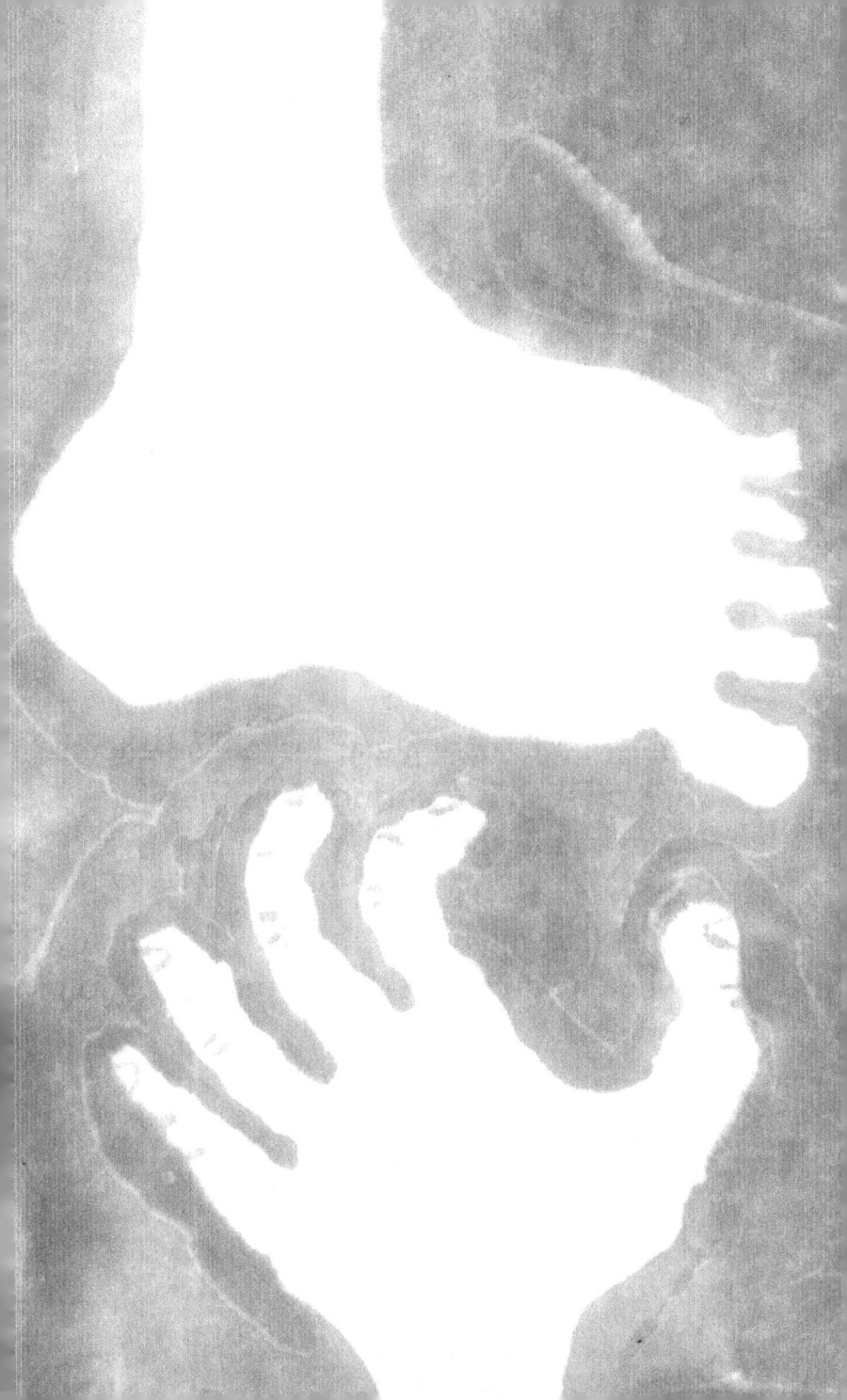

The Balloons And The Pins

The balloons and the pins
are at war again
and as usual the pins are winning –

the deflated bodies
of balloon poodles and bunnies
now lie in their colourful ruins.

But who'll spare a tear for fallen balloons?
Certainly not the triumphant pins.
Maybe the child with the helium eyes

still believing in the promise of birthdays
when next year's balloons regather and rise.

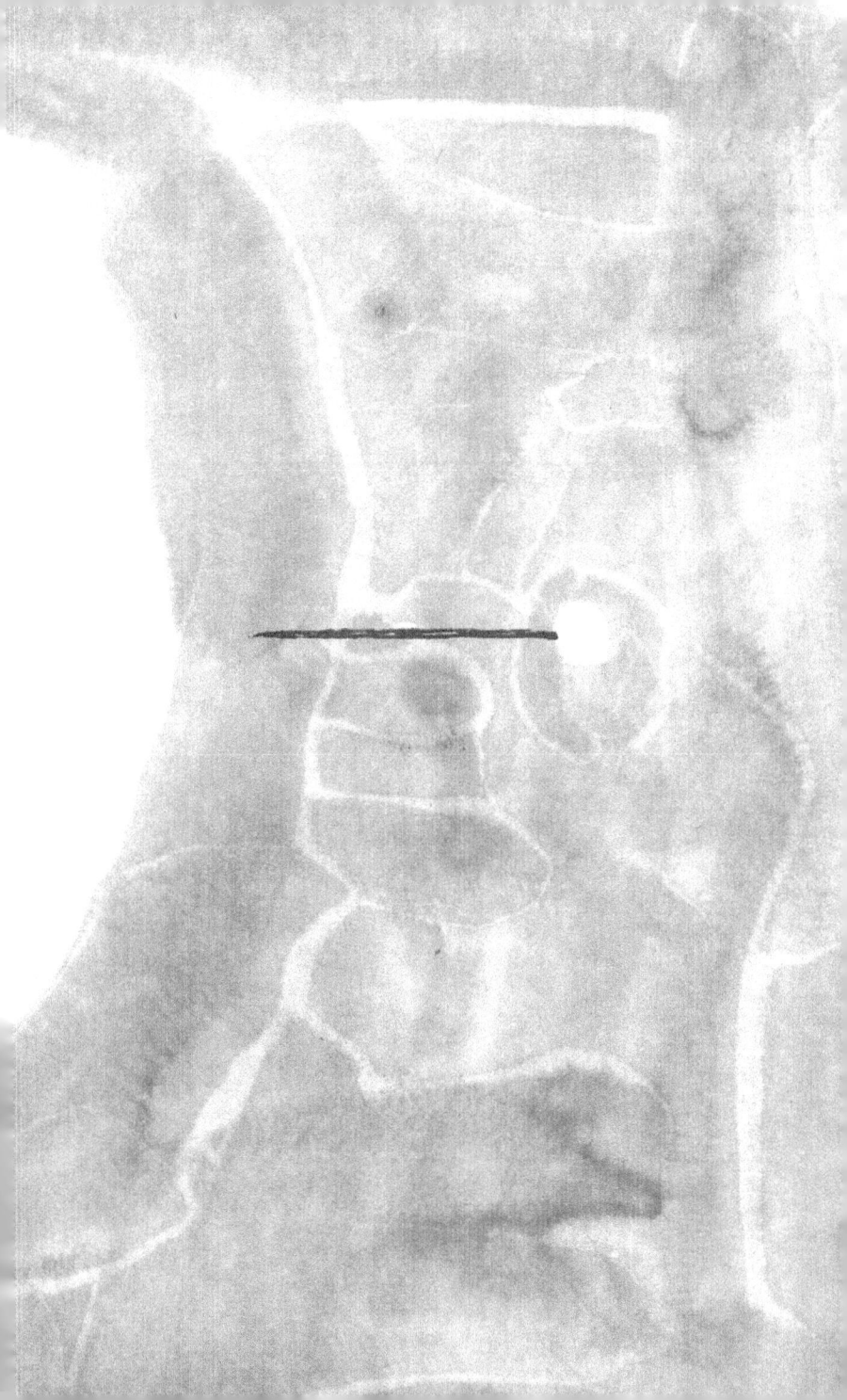

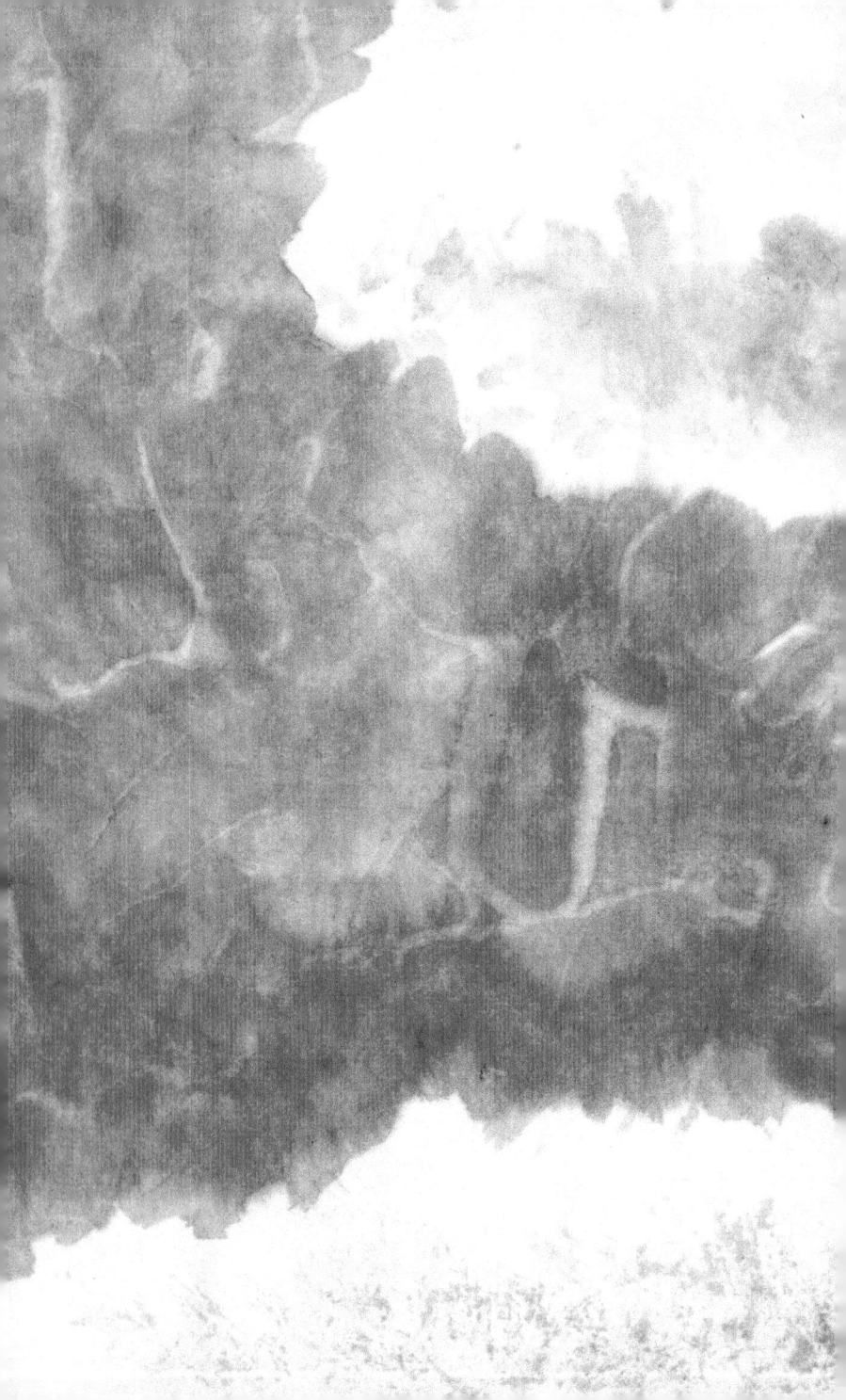

Progress

It takes time
to sling a stone
to fling a spear
to wield a club
to blow a dart
to shoot an arrow
to pull a pistol
to fire a canon

it takes a second
(maybe less)
to press
a button

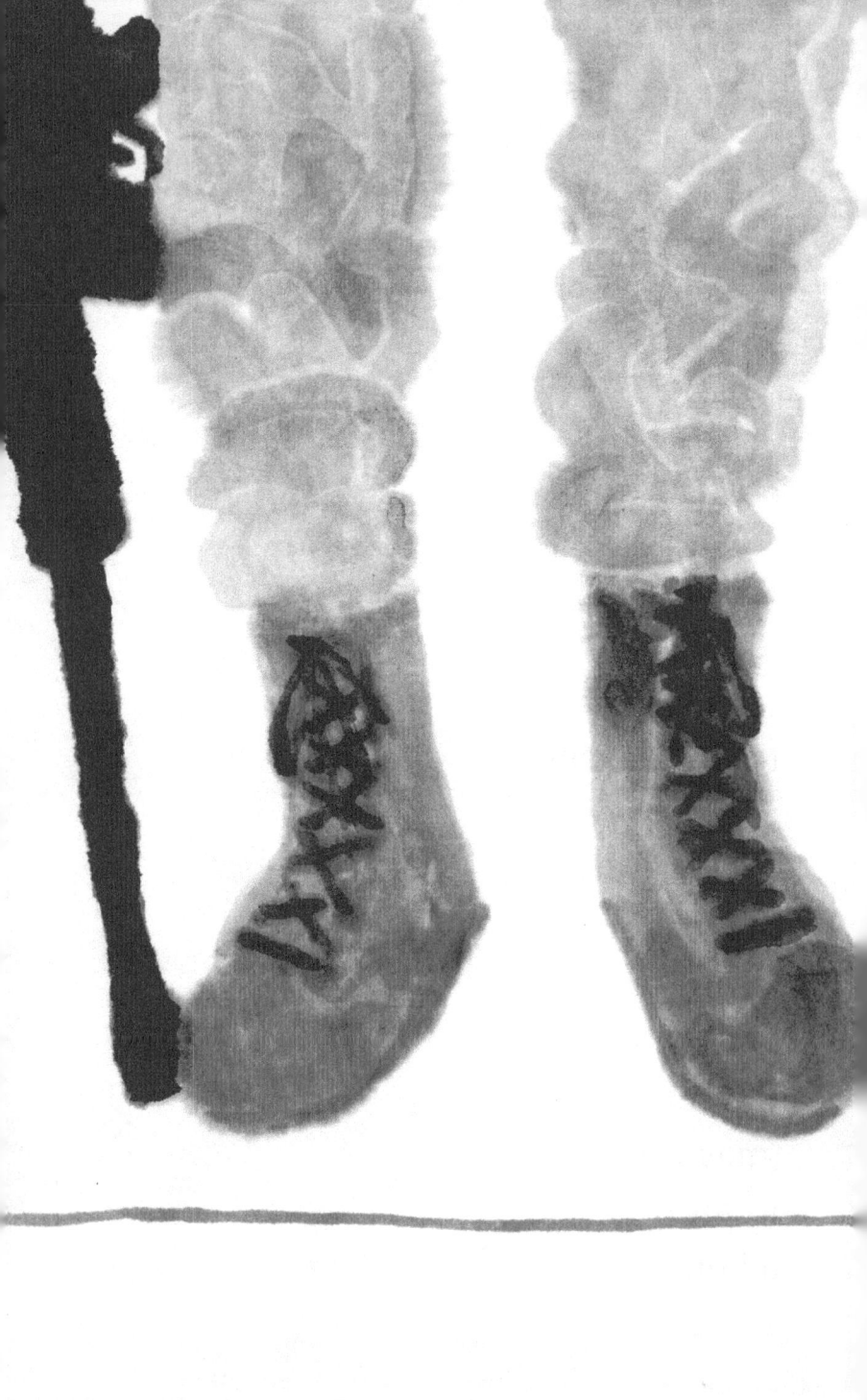

Line

Stand in line
they said
So he did.
Toe the line
they said
So he did.
Sign on
the dotted line
they said
So he did.

Then they sent him
to the frontline
where he learnt
of a thin line
between breathing
and not breathing.

A Single Cry

How strange to wake up
and find world peace has been declared.
You cannot believe your ears.
Has the breaking news on telly been broken far
too soon? Maybe.
But it's on twitter, it's on tweet.
War has been declared obsolete.
No more scenes of speechless desolation
and guns have suddenly gone dumb.
Bullets nestle in the recycling bin.
They can't wait for their new life to begin.
What's the reason for this overnight outbreak
of hugs, kisses, high fives, handshakes?
Don't ask me, mate, but the story goes,
people are now all friends, no more foes.
How will humans cope without enemies?
Well, might there be some in other galaxies?
So all around the globe you hear a single cry:
Unite against all those little green men from the sky.

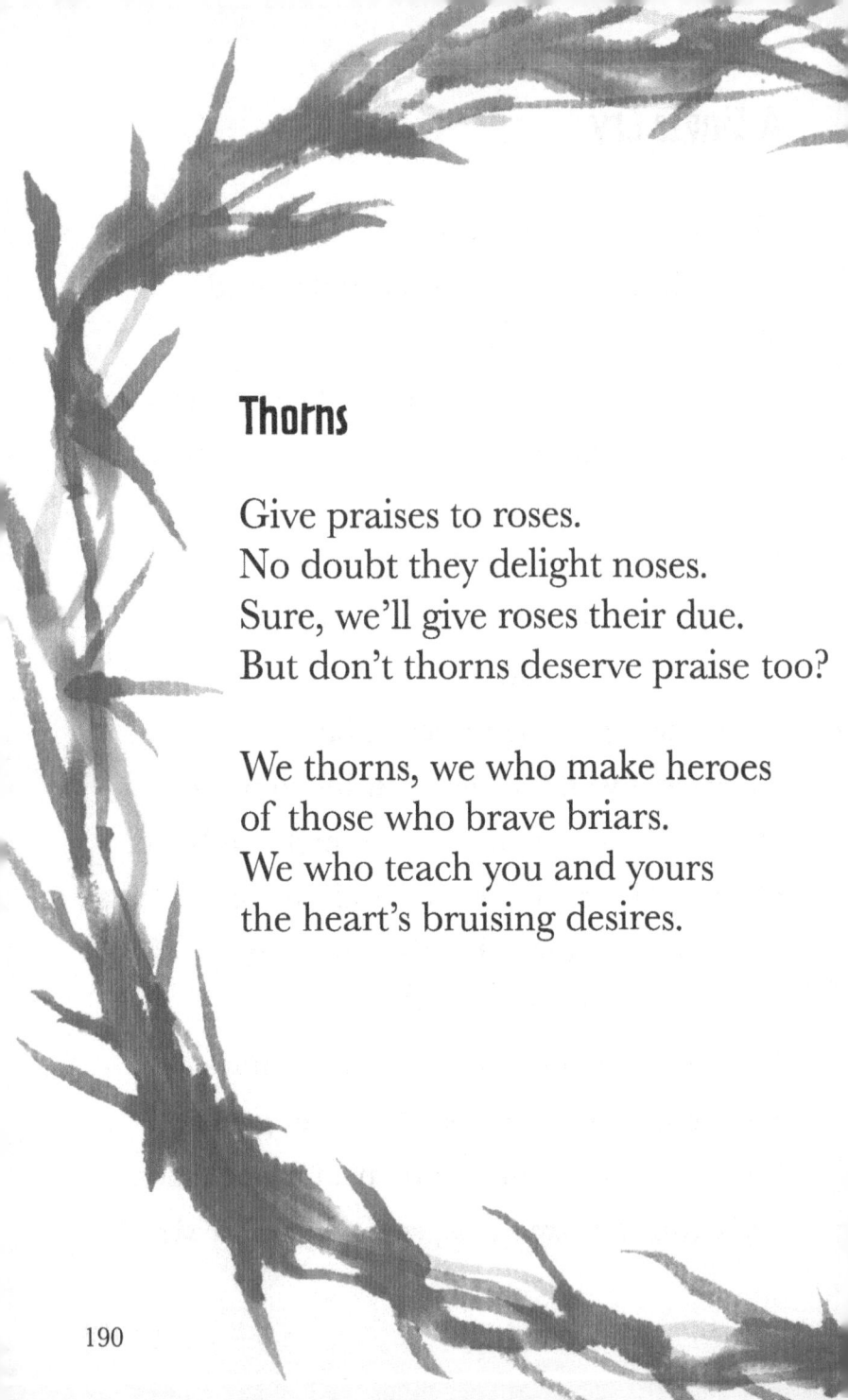

Thorns

Give praises to roses.
No doubt they delight noses.
Sure, we'll give roses their due.
But don't thorns deserve praise too?

We thorns, we who make heroes
of those who brave briars.
We who teach you and yours
the heart's bruising desires.

We thorns, we the ones who bled
from that holy crucified head.
When we thorns became a crown,
where were roses? Nowhere around.

Mosquito

My name is Mosquito.
It's true I'm no Firefly.
I just wouldn't know
how to do a sparkly fly.

This gift I've been denied.
Nor can I, like Butterfly,
become a pretty brooch
on a branch or leaf.

Mosquito's life on planet earth
is sadly all too brief,
(even one week, for what it's worth)
so we intend to make the most

of this very short lifespan
by feasting on the skin of Man.
(Of course, the skin of Woman too
will do nicely, thank you.)

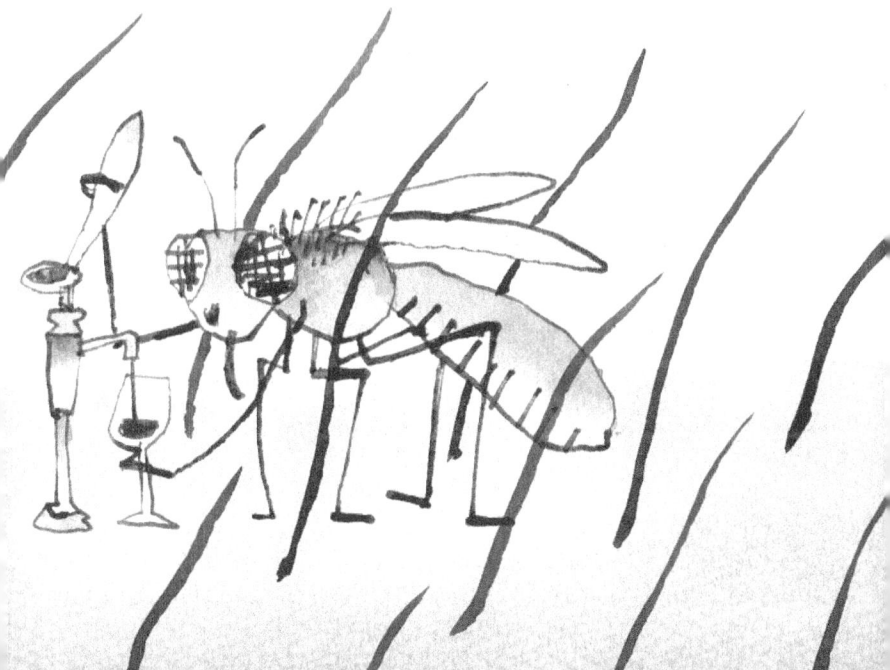

An Off-The-Record Conversation

'Good morning, Butterfly Bush,
did you sleep well last night?'

'Unfortunately not.'

'Sorry to hear you didn't sleep well.
Was it all that raving late night music
that disturbed your leafy slumber?

Or was it that nasty thunder
and lightning from midnight till dawn?
The skies were really chucking it down.'

'Oh no, storms are no bother.
Lightning must do what lightning must do.
Never mind I lose a branch or two.

As for late-night foot-stomping parties,
they're the least of my worries.
I was up all night thinking of butterflies.'

'Butterflies? Why should Butterfly Bush
be losing sleep over butterflies?'

'Because these days they rarely visit me.
I feel like an abandoned granny.
And what's all this about endangered species?

Explain please.'

Three Old Mothers

Old Mother Frost is alive and well –
you can tell by the white on the ground
she's been shaking her feather bed
till snow feathers come tumbling down

Old Mother Thunder is in good spirits –
you can tell by the crackling in the air
and the rumbling in the distance
she's rocking away in her rocking chair

But Old Mother Ozone just sits and stares
into her ultra-violet mirror.
She's losing her hair layer by layer –
Cosmic doing? Or human error?

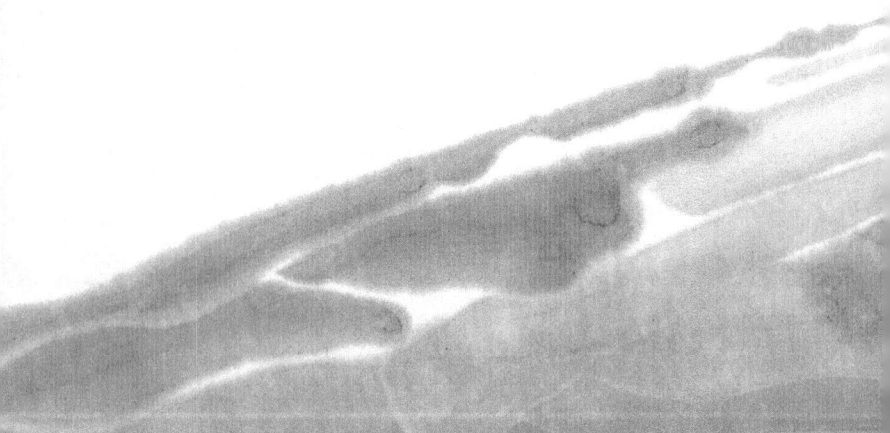

Praying Mantis

Cousin to grasshopper.
Accomplice of gardeners.

You there, at prayer on your knee,
yet armed with front leg choppers.
Unhappy at the end of horsefly or bee
that dares test your poised piety.

Praying Mantis – no stranger
to ancients of the Kalahari
where you are divine rain-bringer.
You who make the grass your altar.

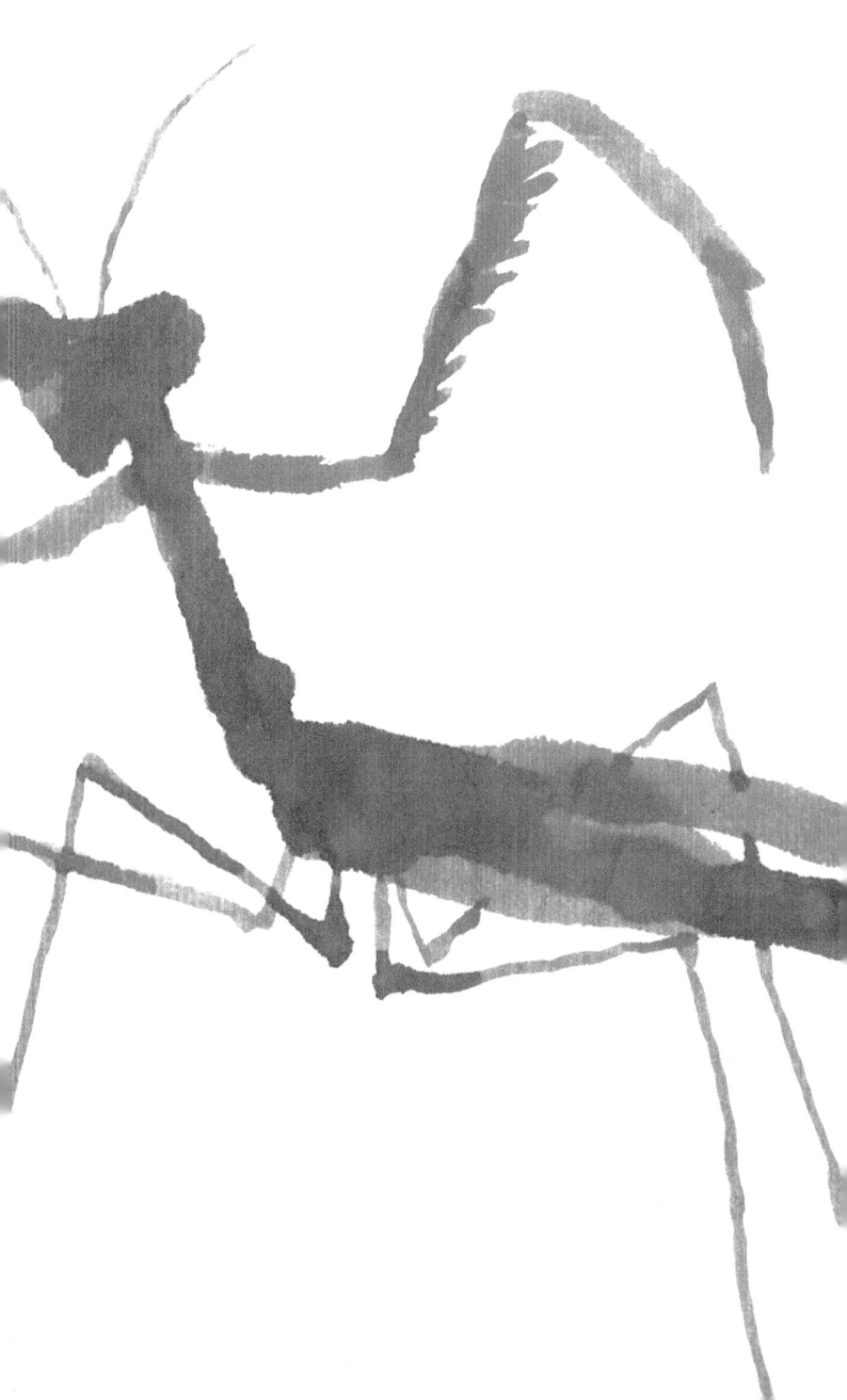

Dear Flower

Dear Flower
Just writing to thank you
for your sudden bright smile
that puts the spring in my morning.
But I should also be thanking
those roots you keep out of sight,
those stems from which you take flight,
not to mention your fluttering
green companions, your leaves of course.
But how could I forget the clouds
that brought you the goodness of rain,
urging you towards blossom,

and the sun that gave its light freely.
O I almost forgot (silly me)
to mention the bats, the butterflies,
the birds, the bees, the bugs,
all for their contribution …
scattering your pollen like children
as the seasons turn.
If it's no trouble, dear flower,
please convey my thanks to all concerned.

Yours sincerely,
Traveller.

More Pointless Questions

Goldfish
goldfish
which glass do you
prefer?
A bowl of glass
or a pond that ripples
when the winds pass?

Little bird
little bird
which do you prefer?
A house of wires
or a branch
that's a stage
for feathered choirs?

Red rose
red rose
which do you prefer?
A vase once used
to contain dry flowers
or a patch of ground
blooming with briars?

Putting such questions
to a goldfish
or a bird
or a rose
is pointless I suppose.

In The Land Where The Dead Bury The Dead

In the land where the dead bury the dead,
speeches are delivered without any words said.

Bones turn up in Sunday-best shrouds and tailored suits.
In church they sing hymns through mouths that stay mute.

They shed no tears yet their eyes are streaming wet.
And the dead are the first to pay their last respects.

They know when the time has come for the living to go
so they gather above to take new arrivals below.

The dead may be cold but they're not cold-hearted.
They always make room for the dear departed.

Later the dead will assemble over tea and biscuits
and liven themselves up with bits of underworld gossip.

But when it's time for me to pop my clogs, I trust
the dead will bury me without too much ceremony and fuss.

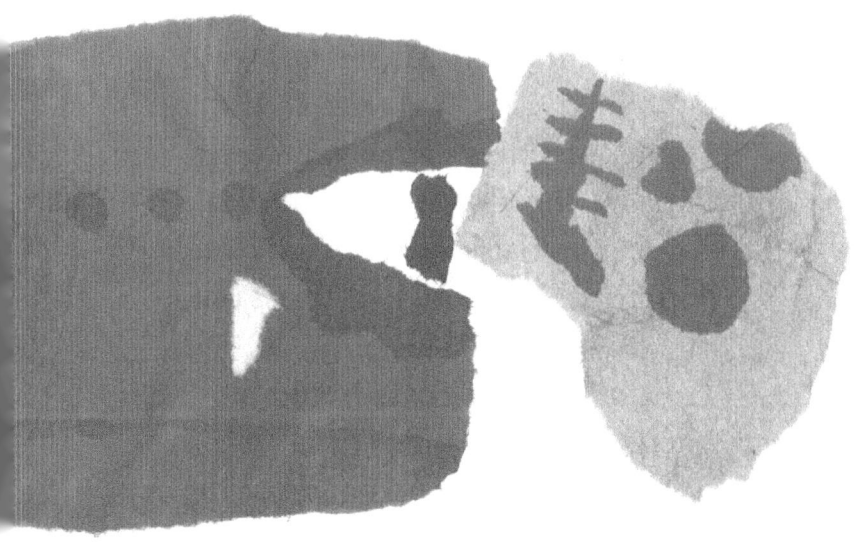

Pushing Up Daisies with Grandpa

Yes, lad, I'll pop me clogs.
I've had a long innings.
I'll kick the bucket.
Sure, I'll snuff it.

I'll cash in me chips.
I'll cross the river Styx.
I'll go Boothill, if I must.
Soon I'll bite the dust.

I'm in God's waiting room.
Departure lounge, if you prefer.
There I'll meet the Grim Reaper
as I make it to my Maker.

Time for me to sing me swan song.
Time to ring up me curtain down.
Pushing up daisies from the Beyond.
Pushing up daisies when I pass on.

Trust me, I'll not cease from toil
when I shove off this mortal coil.
No, I'll be pushing up daisies to the sky.
What's that, lad, did you say die?

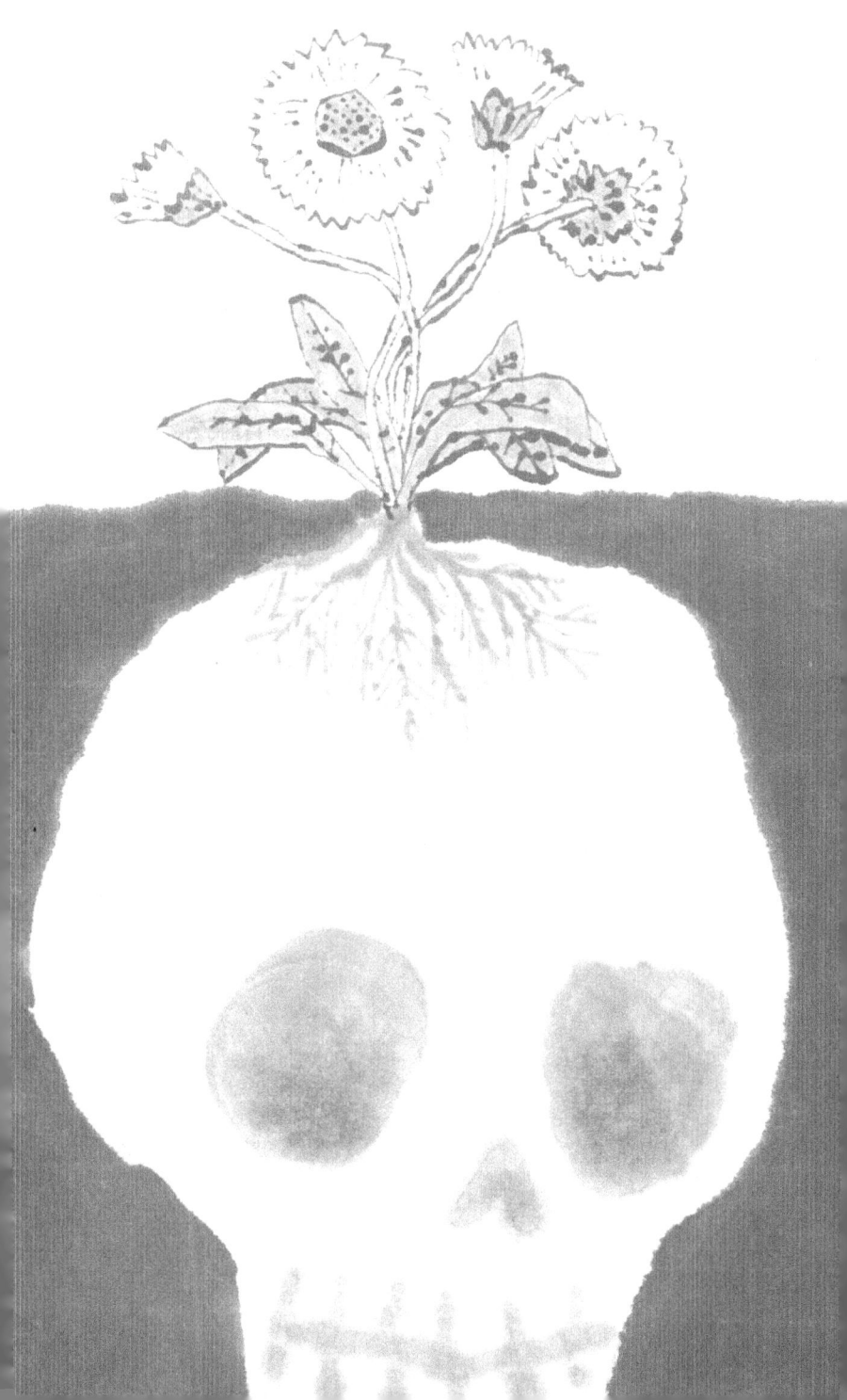

Kangaroo Post

What impresses me most
          about you, Kangaroo

is not your hind-legged boogaloo
          or your forepaw boxer strokes

not your Down Under dreaming
          or your loose-limbed leaping.

No, what impresses me most
          is your miracle envelope –

that pouch through which you post
          your first-class babies to the future.

Dinosaur Meets Electronic Mouse

A dinosaur, just back from extinction,
had centuries of techno inventions to think on.
Still old Brontosaurus kept his blinkers on
as he surveyed the digital revolution.

Brontosaurus stared at electronic mouse.
Electronic mouse stared back at Brontosaurus.
Neither of them had got the other sussed.
Both creatures, you could say, were nonplussed.

Electronic mouse said: 'Don't come too close.
I wouldn't want you to catch my virus.'
Dino replied: 'The last mouse I saw... let me think ...
was the day before I found myself extinct.

Of course, that was millennia before your time
when mice like you possessed what's called a squeak.'
Electronic mouse burrowed into her screen and sighed:
'This Dino has some way to go to becoming a Geek!'

Switched On Without
Final Reminders

Fire-beetles
have their underbelly sensors
for sensing fires miles away

human beetles
also have their smoke detectors
for detecting smoke night or day.

Arctic foxes
have their fur insulators
for keeping winter's bite at bay

human foxes
also have their fitted radiators
for taking the sting out of the chill.

The point of this poem is obvious.
Some creatures pay no electricity bill.

Lost Sheep

I like being the lost sheep.
I don't want to be found
I like being a frisking-free sheep
In unfamiliar ground

I like being the lost sheep
with my head in the clouds
It's liberating to bleat
far from the gullible crowd

I won't return to the fold
I rejoice in being lost,
Who wants to be served cold
as main course with mint sauce?

By Their Fruits Ye Shall Know Them

If humans and animals can be compared:
say a hairy grandpa to a cuddly panda
say a limbo dancer to a wriggly cobra
say a full-o-beans toddler to a frisky hare

then why can't people and fruits be paired
(no pun intended)? So those I find easy
to get along with, I'll call banana-breezy.
Not like those who are pineapple-pricklies.

Yes, the world is full of all fruit-types.
Some are green yet act like they're ripe.
And some look downright rotten outside –
Until you discover their inside.

Then of course you have those who show
the world a tough coconut exterior –
never wanting to appear a softie.
Coconuts with a deep down heart of strawberry.

The Four Footed Olympians

If our four footed-friends competed in sport,
we'd surely see some fit females and blokes.
Giraffe's height would rule the basketball court.
Hippo's weight would boss any wrestling ring.
Leaping Hare a certain gold for triple jumping,
Kangaroo Rat a world record-breaking hurdler.
Polar Bear, of course, born to be a skier.
Don't write off Otter, synchronised swimmer.
Cheetah at a trot would lead the 100 metres.
And Rhino, ah, what a midfield sweeper!
But pity the poor penalty shooter
who must face Octopus for a goalkeeper.
O pity even more the ill-timed referee
who waves a red card to Tiger in a jersey.

The Tomato Says I Do

Who'll be Frankenstein's bride?
Not I
says the corn.
I'm already engaged to the sun.

Who'll be Frankenstein's bride?
Not I
says the wheat.
The wind is my devoted husband.

Who'll be Frankenstein's bride?
Not I
says the mushroom.
Can't you see I'm a fairy's footstool?

Who'll be Frankenstein's bride?
Not I
says the grape.
I'm already wedded to the vine.

Very well, I'll be Frankenstein's bride
says the tomato.
I'll walk him down the aisle

providing of course
that his blushes
were genetically modified.

The Bi-phibians Are Coming

What gives a cow
     Cow-dentity?
Is it the horn
or the rolling laidback moo?

What gives an owl
     Owl-dentity?
Is it the hoot
or the night-time point of view?

What gives a dog
     Dog-dentity?
Is it the bark
or the welcome wag of tail?

What gives a cat
     Cat-dentity
Is it the purr
or the caterwauling wail?

What gives a bee
     Bee-dentity?

Is it the buzz
or the shimmer of wing?

What gives a fish
        Fish-dentity?
Is it the scale
or the fingerprint fin?

What gives me
        I-dentity
Is it the tone of skin
or the colour of speech?

What makes the you in me reach
out to the me somewhere in you?
Since I'm the offspring of sea and land
then that must make me Bi-phibian

Delighted, my friend, to meet you.
Do you by chance tick Bi-phibian too?

Taking Sides

What religion
does the rain follow?
It descends with little
thought of litany
or bended knee,
yet rain fills the air
with drops of prayer.

Which language
does the thunder speak?
Its expressive claps
need no translator
for all who take shelter
from a storm's rolling outburst.
Thunder respects no borders.

And those birds
that are morning's chorus?
Whose side are they on?
Are they for us or for them?
Those birds that warble
the same anthem
for enemy as well as friend?

Among The Hairyboos And Smoothyboos

The Hairyboos were hairy, the Smoothyboos smooth.
But they lived side by side and were never rude.
Strangely, their language had no word for hate,
they called a stranger like myself *afar-heart-mate*.
These two undiscovered races spoke the same tongue.
Their national anthem sounds fun (even in translation).

'Hairyboo, Smoothyboo, we same people.
Two different rivers, one ripple.
Forward Hairyboo, Forward Smoothyboo,
Ever onward, ever tickety-boo.'

And you'd think they sing standing to attention.
But no, they sing their anthem lying down
in what's known as the circle of one heartbeat,
while the men and women stare at each other's feet.
This is an ancient tradition (or so I've been told)
for they say to ponder the feet is to ponder the soul.

The Hairyboos are worshippers of bristles and fur,
and treat as sacred the coconut's hairy shell.
The Smoothyboos, on the other hand, pray to pebbles.
And in every egg or ball they see a miracle.
These almost extinct tribes have an old expression:
If you don't have an enemy, why invent one?

The Encounter

How lovely to meet a man
who said he'd come from nowhere.
I'd always been fed the view
that everyone comes from somewhere.

He greeted me, as the locals do,
with a down-to-earth Goodie day.
He said he'd just arrived from nowhere
and did not intend to stay.

Just passing through, just passing through.
Can't wait to get back to nowhere.
Don't know how you folks from somewhere
can cope with being in one hemisphere.

Homo Ambi-thumb-trous

In times when eyes stare
into eyes of mobile phones
and ears imprison ears
in their *don't-talk-to-me zones*

I've seen folk texting
with their left thumb
I've seen folk texting
with their right thumb.

Now don't get me wrong,
I'm not hi-tech dumb.
But those texting with two thumbs
(at one go) leave me spellbound.

Roll over *Homo Erectus.*
Make way for Homo Ambi-thumb-trous.

Einstein, The Girl Who Hated Maths
Notes

p.24 Ishango Bone: Excavated in Africa and thought to be the oldest mathematical object, this fossilised baboon bone dates back more than 8,000 years. Some say its notches formed a counting device and might also have been used by African women for counting the phases of the moon. The Ishango Bone is now housed in the Institute for Natural Sciences in Brussels.

p.34 Quipu: Though the Incas had no written language, they used the quipu (meaning knot) for keeping records and accounts. Knots on cords of different colours became a filing system.

p.38 Archimedes was concerned with finding out how much weight a body loses when submerged in water. During one of his legendary baths more than 2,000 years ago, the story goes he found the answer and ran naked through the streets of Syracuse in Sicily shouting 'Eureka! Eureka!' ('I found it! I found it!')

p.56 German mathematician Georg Cantor (1845-1918) explored levels of infinity based on a theory of 'sets and sub-sets'. In case anyone finds this theory unsettling, remember Cantor said, 'My theory is solid. I have drawn its principles from the first cause of all created things.'

p.56 Indian mathematician Srinivasa Ramanujan (1887-1920) taught himself mathematics by borrowing books from the library. He performed his calculations on a slate and left behind hundreds of intriguing formulas in notebooks. For Ramanujan, 'the universe is a product of zero and infinity.'

p.58 Seventeenth-century French mathematician Pierre de Fermat wrote in his copy of Arithmetica, 'I have found a truly marvellous proof which this margin is too narrow to contain.' This proof for a certain equation was to keep the best mathematical minds busy for more than 350 years. Andrew Wiles, a Cambridge-born mathematician, is credited with solving this puzzle, famously known as 'Fermat's Last Theorem'.

p.60 The Magic Square contains numbers arranged in such a way that whether you add from left to right or right to left, up down, or diagonally, the total is always the same. According to one Chinese legend, the Magic Square was revealed to the Emperor Yu through the markings on the back of a magic turtle.

p.69 Googol is the number one followed by a hundred zeros (or ten to the hundredth power). According to mathematical legend, American mathematician Dr Edward Kasner was given the word by his young nephew.

p.72 Nobel-Prize winning German-American physicist and mathematician Albert Einstein (1879-1955) also played the violin, which he said helped him with his theory of relativity. One of his teachers described the young Einstein as 'stupid'. The older Einstein once said, 'Do not worry about your difficulties in mathematics, I can assure you that mine are still greater.'

Since it took me three attempts to pass my O-level maths, I would have been completely googolplexed without the help of a number of books. Among those I'm grateful to are:

The Universal History of Numbers From Prehistory to the Invention of the Computer by Georges Ifrah, translated from the French by David Bellos, E.F. Harding, Sophie Wood, and Ian Mark (Harvill Press 1998)

The Magic of Mathematics by Theoni Pappas (Wide World Publishing/Tetra 1994)

The Mystery of Numbers by Annemarie Schimmel (Oxford University Press 1993)

The Man Who Loved Only Numbers by Paul Hoffman (Fourth Estate 1998)

Numbers: The Universal Language by Denis Guedj (Gallimard 1996), English translation by Lory Frankel (Harry H. Abrams 1997)

Fermat's Last Theorem – Unlocking the Secret of an Ancient Mathematical Problem by Amir D Aczel (Four Walls Eight Windows 1996)

The Story of Numbers – How Mathematics Has Shaped Civilisation by John McLeish (Fawcett Columbine 1991)

The Crest of the Peacock – Non-European Roots of Mathematics by George Gheverghese Joseph (Penguin Books 1992)

Zero – The Biography of a Dangerous Idea by Charles Seife (Souvenir Press 2000).

And to Satoshi's mind-teasing e-mails.

Hello H2O
Notes

p.88 In the plant world, a lot of 'cloning' goes on. A twig that is planted in the ground, or grafted to the branch of another tree, is known as a 'clone' from the Greek word for twig. In July 1996 a sheep was scientifically reproduced in this manner. Dolly, the world's first cloned mammal, was born. Dolly went on to have six lambs and died in February 2003. The debate continues whether it is right or not to clone mammals.

p.94 Two thousand years ago, the Chinese were already experimenting with compasses, first using a lodestone carved in the shape of a ladle. Later they used a magnetised needle and the 'southpointing fish' made from a flat leaf of iron. It was the Arabs who introduced the Chinese idea to the Western world. Without this method of 'navigating by needle', many European voyages would not have been possible.

p.110 Leonardo da Vinci was born in 1452 in Vinci, Italy. He not only played the lute and painted the famous Mona Lisa. He also spent days dissecting bodies to discover the secrets of anatomy. After his death in 1519, he left behind thousands of pages of notebooks, filled with sketches and ideas for inventions, some of them even looking like modern-day helicopters and scuba diving equipment. But you'll need a mirror to read his notebooks, for Leonardo wrote in mirror-writing.

p.116 Galileo was born in 1564 in Pisa, Italy. Apparently, he wasn't too keen on science at school but he grew up to be a legendary skywatcher. He also used his telescope as a microscope and was fascinated to see 'flies which look as big as lambs'. Even when he became blind in 1637, he was still making discoveries in astronomy. He was persecuted for his belief that the earth went around the sun. He died at the age of seventy-eight, knowing that he was right.

p.122 D.N.A, or deoxyribonucleic acid if you prefer, has been described as a sort of alphabet we inherit in a molecule that stores information that makes us who we are. This D.N.A molecule connects us to our furthest ancestors and its shape has been compared to a ladder or two coiled together snakes. Among peoples

such as the Aborigines and the Amazonian Indians, there is a belief
that ancestral spirits descend a ladder and that all creation was the work of
a 'cosmic serpent.'

p.132 George Washington Carver was born around 1865 in Missouri, U.S.A.
during the time of slavery. As a boy, he was always curious about plants, and
went on to be the first African-American member of the faculty at Iowa State
College. As an agricultural scientist, or 'plant doctor', he was best known for
his experiments with peanuts, using them for soil improvement and even for
household items like soap and shoe polish. His face appeared on a stamp and a
coin. The farm that was his birthplace is a national monument. He died in 1943.

p.140 Physicist Madame Curie was born Marya Sklodowska in Poland in 1867.
She won two Nobel Prizes for both Physics and Chemistry – one in 1903 shared
with her Chemist husband, Pierre Curie, and one in 1911 for her discovery
of polonium and radium. When she first saw Radium in the shed she used as
a laboratory, she said 'it was really a lovely sight and always new to us. The
glowing tubes looked like faint fairy lights.' But this luminous element is also
known to have harmful effects. Marie died in 1934 of an aplastic anemica, a
sickness which is believed to be the result of handling radium without protection.

p.144 Any queries about Quarks, especially quirky queries, are best addressed
to Quarks themselves. But you'll have to travel to the very centre of a nucleus to
meet these shifty particles that came to the attention of scientists in the 1960s.

p.146 For American Indians, plants possessed a living spirit and were nature's
healers. The Indians knew that the willow was a good painkiller long before
western science discovered it as the 'aspirin tree'.

Among the books which have been beacons in a sea of facts as well as wonder,
I owe my thanks to: Isaac Asimov's *New Guide to Science* (Penguin); Peter James
and Nick Thorpe's *Ancient Inventions* (Michael O'Mara Books Limited); Marcel
Griaule's *Conversations With Ogotmmeli* (Oxford University Press); David Peat's
Blackfoot Physics (4th Estate); Lisa Yount's *Black Scientists* (Facts on File Inc.); Dava
Sobel's *Galileo's Daughter* (4th Estate); Oliver Sacks' *Uncle Tungsten* (Picador);
Frances Ashcroft's *Life at the Extremes* (Flamingo); Jeremy Narby's *The Cosmic
Serpent* (Pheonix)
And my thanks to the Hodder Team and as ever to Satoshi Kitamura.

John Agard was born in Guyana and came to Britain in 1977. He is one of the most exciting poets writing in the English language today and in in 2012 he was award the prestigious Queen's Gold Medal for Poetry. His poem 'Half-Caste' is on the AQA English GCSE syllabus, and every year he tours the country performing with other top poets for GCSE students. Alongside his poetry, John has written and performed his own plays and written for venues such as Little Angel Theatre and the Glyndebourne Festival. He lives in Sussex and is married to Grace Nichols, herself a leading poet.

Photo credit: Motoko Matsuda

Satoshi Kitamura is an award-winning children's picture book author and illustrator who currently lives and works in Japan. He is a self-taught artist and a lover of comic books.

@satoshikitamura6789

Winner of the Eleanor Farjeon Award 2016

JOHN AGARD

half-
caste

'yu mean when tchaikovsky
sit down at
dah piano
an mix a black key
wid a white key
is a half-caste symphony'

Issues of race and identity are explored by
one of the UK's top performance poets in
this classic collection.

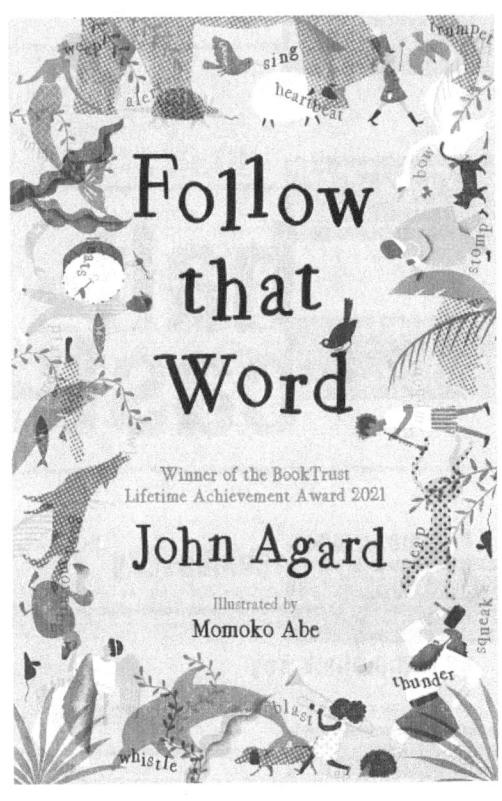

Follow that Word

Winner of the BookTrust
Lifetime Achievement Award 2021

John Agard

Illustrated by
Momoko Abe

A collection of riotously funny poems
celebrating imagination and demonstrating
the true diversity of language.

An uplifting and playful poem in picture
book form, perfect for younger readers.